HUMAN LOGIC
AND THE
THEATER of
EVERYDAY LIFE

HUMAN LOGIC

and the

THEATER *of* EVERYDAY LIFE

David Thomas, PhD

For my parents

Table of Contents

Acknowledgments

In a sense, this book began in 1983 with the development of "The Five Levels" schematic and then later, in 1992 and over the years since, with the development and testing of the Ethics of Human Development Training Program.

For their support, feedback, and encouragement during the development of the ethics training program and/or the writing of this book, I would like to thank Doug Paterson, Don Jennings, Jay Williamson, Terry Kempf, David Shrader, Dan Wilkins, Keith and Ocoee Miller, Gordon Becker, Phil Minkin, John Thomas, Beth Garrett, Charlie Hill, Daniel Dancer, R. Ross Gipple, Verne Varona, Nancy Kelly, Richard Goldstein, Thomas Reed, Warren Zweiback, Jon Levin, John Miller, William Tuttle, Donald Stilson, Gil Wilshire, and Paula Ziegman.

There have been several individuals in leadership positions who believed in the value of the training program (then called The Ethics of Choice Training Program) and who invited it into their organizations. Without their belief in the content of the program and their willingness to experiment with it inside their organizations, the program could not have evolved. In this regard, I wish to thank Richard and Phyllis Gilliland, Jane Matheson, Cheryl Doherty, Pat Cavill, Dean Fixsen, Karen Blasé, Gene Klein, Bob Vodica, Scot Adams, Vicki Maca, Jeffrey Johnson, Jay Williamson, Howard Shrier, Kathleen Doyle-Linden, and Judy Mallory.

Though numerous writers and thinkers are acknowledged in the endnotes, there are certain scholars whose work has been of particular importance to me: R. Buckminster Fuller, John David Garcia, E. F. Schumacher, Ken Wilber, Bruce Wilshire, James Carse, Ernest Becker, B. F. Skinner, Steven Hayes, Montrose Wolf, William M. Tuttle, Jr., and L. Keith Miller.

My heartfelt thanks to R. Ross Gipple for his kind support in making the completion of an earlier version of this book possible.

In many respects, I wrote this book for my family. It is dedicated to my parents, Burt and Betty Thomas, but with my extended family, my children, and their families very much in mind. Dwain and Lora Dean Smith, Louise Hawkins, Beth Garrett and her long-time friend, Blake Elliott, Nick and Katie Lane and their children, Thomas and Nickolas, Luke and Lacy Garrett and Luke's son, Tyson, and John and Ann Thomas and their children, David, Laura, Jane, and Mary Kate. All have given me their time, love, and support throughout my life. And my daughters and their families, about whom I cannot say enough: Blake Thomas and Alistair Wandesforde, and their children Louise, Gordon, Freddy, and Vera, and Chesley Thomas and Matt Kudlacz, and their children, Kate and Johnny.

Finally, I want to thank my wife and life partner, Paula Ziegman. What she has contributed to this work (and to me) is difficult to put into words. She has my enduring love and respect. I thank her for the support and understanding she extended to me during the writing of this book and for the ongoing dialogue that enriched many sections of the book and continues to enrich my life.

David Thomas, PhD
July 2025

"What I am is a matter of what I… can make
of my situation now…"

—Bruce Wilshire
Role Playing and Identity

Preface

> "For even higher than the life of art is the art of life. And ethics
> is the lore of the art of life."[1]
> —Will Durant
> *The Mansions of Philosophy*

PURPOSE

The purpose of this book is to discuss the role of ethics in the making and maturing of the self. We are made and increasingly enlightened—I want to say—depending on how we deal with the tests of heart and mind that come our way. Perhaps this is saying the obvious, something everyone knows. How else are we made and matured? Regardless, and perhaps all the better if it is obvious, that is the idea at the heart of this book.

HOW ARE WE TO VIEW LIFE?

When I was young, Roy Rogers was everything to me. He was my favorite cowboy. When he died (1998), people looked back to a time when Roy filled the big screen and, later, came into America's homes with his Saturday morning television show.

According to one commentator, Roy's films filled a vacuum of which most people were unaware: These were B movies starring a singing cowboy, but mostly, and above all, they were morality plays, providing far more guidance to children of troubled families than most people might imagine.[2]

How are we to view life? It's an important question since how we view life can affect our approach to it. Perspective is everything, they say.

For Picasso, life was a miracle, a marvel to behold. For the writer Conrad Aiken, it was a comic pilgrimage, an attempt to get somewhere—wherever that somewhere was—through efforts both heartfelt and bungling. And then there are those, far too many to credit, for whom life is a dream, full of meaning, perhaps, but with a will and logic all its own.

For the purposes of this book, life is (or is also) a morality play (not unlike one of Roy's movies) with each of us cast as actors in the play. With this view, choice is emphasized—the role of choice in shaping character and in moving the play along.

The overall assumption is that each of us is in our own morality play and that it lasts a lifetime; and, at another level, that there is the morality play that is the human drama itself. In both cases, the presumption is that the script is not written ahead of time but is written as we go.

With this view, the role of ethics is placed front and center. The "lore" that guides us. To be clear, however, the ethics discussed in this book are not business ethics, corporate ethics, medical ethics, or environmental ethics, as important as these topics are. Rather, the focus here is on what we will call the ethics of human development, the ethics that embody *human logic.*

HUMAN LOGIC

I first became aware of the notion of "human logic" via a quote from Edwin M. Epstein of the Walter A. Haas School of Business at the University of California–Berkeley, along the lines of: "The Japanese word for ethics, *rinri,* translates roughly as 'human logic' or the 'way of being human.'" Later, I discovered Watsuji Tetsuro's *Rinrigaku (Ethics in Japan).* Tetsuro writes: ethics are "the way human beings truly become human beings."[3]

Human logic—the way human beings truly become human beings—is discussed throughout the book and given detail in the twelve ethics of human development (Part II). However, that discussion can be foreshadowed by a return to Roy and to the presumption of life as morality play—miracle, dream, pilgrimage, yes, but morality play as well.

When the character Roy played in the movies righted wrong, the community benefited. But so, too, did Roy's character. His character (let us presume) became wiser, stronger, more conscious and aware of how to deal with similar situations in the future. The self serves the whole but is also served in return, educated, let's say... to a degree, enlightened.[4] That is ethics as human logic. "The gift is to the giver and comes back most to him [or her] . . . It cannot fail"[5] is the way Whitman put it.

TWO ASSUMPTIONS

There are two assumptions required for the discussion that follows. The first is that we want for ourselves the realization of our full potential as human beings. Psychologist Carl Rogers wrote: "There is in every organism, at whatever level, an underlying flow of movement toward constructive fulfillment of its inherent possibilities."[6] That is the first assumption: *we want for ourselves the constructive fulfillment of our inherent possibilities,*[7] self-realization, to use another term.

The second assumption is that *ethical conduct facilitates the fulfillment of inherent possibilities.* In one sense, of course, ethical conduct *is* the fulfillment of inherent possibilities. It is one of the ends toward which we are aiming as we develop; namely, the capacity to behave ethically across all situations and settings. But ethical conduct, while an end unto itself, is also a means, calling on us to *identify and undo* our hardened habits of thinking and doing if those habits hold us back when principle calls us in another direction.

To put it another way, through our effort to behave ethically we are brought into contact with the resistances within ourselves with which we must wrestle if we are to unlock and develop our potential as human beings—not just our potential to behave ethically, but our potential (if this is not saying the same thing) to live and work and love creatively.

Assumption #2: Through our effort to behave ethically, we gain self-knowledge. We see what we have made of ourselves to date, and we see, as well, perhaps, the challenges ahead if we are to make more of ourselves.

There are five parts to this book.

>**Part I: Human Development & the Yellow Brick Road.** Part I provides a map of the developmental possibilities available to each of us as human beings, from the innocence and dependence of the infant to the wisdom and independence of the fully mature adult. These levels of development suggest the direction in which we evolve and mature, aided increasingly by conduct in accord with the ethics of human development.

>**Part II: Human Logic and the Ethics of Human Development.** Part II presents the ethics of human development, the ethics that give body and detail to the notion of human logic. In explaining these ethics, the focus largely is on life in organizations. The presumption is that we are involved with organizations throughout our lives, beginning (and ending, perhaps) with the family, and that how we choose to behave in these organizations affects both our development and the development of our organizations.

>**Part III: Dilemmas from Work & Everyday Life.** Part III provides examples of situations that present us with ethical dilemmas, the tests of heart and mind on which development depends.

>**Part IV: Consciousness, Valued Behavior & the Center of Gravity.** Part IV focuses first, and very briefly, on consciousness, in particular, on the importance of the ideas/values we have and hold in mind; second, on "valued behavior", on its importance in the face of the pain and suffering that are an inevitable part of life; and finally, on the way in which our behavior impacts the "center of gravity" in self, organization, and society.

>**Part V: The Theater of Change.** Part V provides a brief overview of the training program developed to teach the ethics of human development and continues with a consideration of the larger forces affecting development. Concerning those forces, there is, on the one hand, the fear that encourages us to settle for things as they are, and, on the other hand, there is the "ontological longing" for greater self-realization.

"Higher than the life of art is the art of life" (Durant). But what is the art of life? From the point of view of this book, it is the meeting of what is given ethically, creatively (and compassionately, if that is not implied). To practice this art, as with any art, is to get better at it. Our capacity expands because, increasingly, we know what is required both ethically and for art's sake.

But what's in it, we might ask, for the would-be life artist? Doing good in the world is perhaps reward enough, yes, but *experientially speaking,* the feeling that accompanies the effort to live ethically/artfully... what's in it for the life artist? Philosopher Bruce Wilshire wrote: "Nothing is more powerfully impelling and moving than is our own *well functioning...*" (emphasis added). Perhaps that is enough, to experience ourselves as well functioning. Though Wilshire goes on to say that he prefers the term "humming".[9] Let us make that assumption: the life artist experiences herself as well functioning *(humming)* when engaged in the art of life...not always but reward, motivation, and sustenance enough when it occurs.

Part I

*Human Development
and the Yellow Brick Road*

"In the whole of philosophy, there is no subject in greater disarray than ethics. Anyone asking the professors of ethics for the bread of guidance or how to conduct himself, will receive not even a stone but just a torrent of 'opinions.' With very few exceptions, they embark upon an investigation into ethics without any prior clarification of the purpose of human life on Earth. It is obviously impossible to decide what is good or bad, right or wrong, virtuous or evil, without an idea of purpose: Good for what? To raise the question of purpose has been called 'the naturalistic fallacy'—virtue is its own reward! None of the great teachers of mankind would have been satisfied with such an evasion. If a thing is said to be good but no one can tell me what it is good for, how can I be expected to take any interest in it? If our guide, our annotated Map of Life, cannot show us where The Good is situated and how it can be reached, it is worthless."[1]

—E. F. Schumacher
A Guide for the Perplexed

THE FIVE LEVELS SCHEMATIC

Figure 1 presents a schematic depicting the five developmental possibilities available to each of us as human beings. These five levels can be considered way stations on what L. Frank Baum in his book *The Wizard of Oz* called the Yellow Brick Road,[2] a metaphor used throughout the book. The schematic is a map.[3] It is not science or documented fact. It is an attempt to conjure a feeling for the developmental possibilities available to each of us in the course of a lifetime. It is provided in accord with Schumacher's requirement to show where The Good is situated.

Read the schematic from left to right, row by row, to get a sense of each level as it is defined by the relationship of the descriptors to one another. The levels are arbitrary. They blend into one another and, certainly, there could be more or fewer levels. Even so, there is a direction and a maturation that is mapped.

NOTE: As indicated above, the Five Levels schematic is not science. The stages are not based on field surveys or on psychological testing, nor are they considered synonymous with unfolding physiological structures. Rather, the Five Levels schematic is simply a way of mapping developmental possibility through the ordering of common or everyday terms.

When first developed, I was aware of only one other similar system. Since that time, I have become aware of many such systems. What I have concluded over the years, having reviewed many developmental systems (some scientific and far more detailed), is that the Five Levels schematic maps adequately the territory for many a would-be traveler.

--- *The Five Levels of Human Development* ---

	I	II	III	IV	V
The Five Levels:	No Mind →	Hive Mind →	Heroic Mind →	Poetic Mind →	Mature Mind
Group Descriptor:	"the innocents"	"the robots"	"the self-actualizers"	"the relativists"	"the free"
What They Mind:	infant or damaged genes	what other people think	themselves	their world (their reality)	evolutionary principle
Governing Psychology:	approach-avoidance	modeling/ imitation	decision makers/ goal-oriented operatives	creative role players	synergetic
Technological Metaphor:	"switch"	"mirror"	"thermostat"	"lamp"	"transformer"
What They Seek:	satisfaction	acceptance	self-esteem	rhyme & reason	unity/fusion
Level of Biological Organization:	cellular	autonomic	somatic	psychosomatic	psychic
Kind of Animal:	amoeba	termite/ lemming	eagle	dolphin	human being
Belief Style:	pre-believers	believers	disbelievers	suspension of disbelief(ers)	beyond belief
Where They Are Going:	nowhere	where the herd takes them	their way	"with the flow"	the stars
Relationship to "System":	system drains	system followers	system rebelers	system makers	system transcenders
What They Harvest:	survival	security	territory	vision	soul
Developmental Imperative:	→	Grow Up! →	Go For It! →	Cultivate the Imagination! →	Turn the Fool Loose!

Here, in brief, is the developmental sequence depicted in the Five Levels schematic. Over the course of a lifetime, given persistence, given sufficient guidance, given good fortune, we grow and mature as persons, we evolve from...

> -- a self just beginning to form for which the need for biological survival rules the day (Level I)

> -- to a self formed through the units of family, community, and local culture, a self that is conscious of other selves and in search of the acceptance and validation that other selves provide (Level II)

> -- to a self more fully individualized, self-directed, no longer a believer in the party line but a rebel with a cause, a cause that may or may not benefit others but which, at base, is intended to secure a sense of place, worth, and self-esteem (Level III)

> -- to a self with greater mindfulness, imaginatively engaged, actively working to undo the hardening habits of thinking and doing that obstruct opportunity, understanding, the flow of experience (Level IV)

> -- to a self at the top of its game—integrated, playful, capable of service to the largest of possible motives; a self that through discipline has won its freedom, the freedom to transcend the concerns of all previous levels if duty and service to life so require (Level V)

And lest this sequence appear too linear, not like life as we know it, we should quickly remember that development is neither certain nor continuous. We get stuck, sometimes captured by our hardened habits. We drift.

In some relationships, for example, we may operate predominately from Level II, expressing the values and views of the other person, living their "program", their approval and acceptance vital to us for whatever reason. In other relationships, we may operate predominately from Level III, interacting with others to further our goals, others a means to our ends. And in still other relationships, perhaps, we operate predominately from Level V, with love and regard for what is best for us and the other person over the long run.

Similarly, in some situations, we are ill at ease, dependent, waiting for others to define our experience, feeling (rightly or wrongly) as though our very survival is at stake. In other situations, we are confident, at ease with ourselves, able to interact creatively with what is before us (Levels IV/V).

Only on average are we located at a specific developmental level. Our task, developmentally speaking, is to rise above our established "norm" as best we can to see if a higher standard is within reach.

TRAUMA, ABUSE, SHOCK

It's also the case that our development, however continuous it may have been, can be severely disrupted, even brought to a halt.

Consider, for example, the abused child. Developmental trajectory is established in the early years of life. With nurturing and care, this trajectory is optimized, the child made ready for the requirements of Levels II, III, and beyond. With abuse, however, or neglect of whatever sort, the trajectory can be inhibited, perhaps in ways that remain undetected for years. The individual may discover later in life a lack of readiness for the increasingly subtle requirements of adulthood. It is possible to repair this damage, to put right the trajectory, but not without difficulty. The discipline and commitment that is required of the individual, and the art, acceptance, and unconditional love that are so helpful to the repair process, are not altogether common. Without these ingredients, however, the distortions imposed by childhood abuse can exert their influence for a lifetime. This is what the French philosopher Sartre was alluding to when he said, "Childhood decides"[4]; not the whole truth, but a chilling sentence given the truth it does contain.

Similarly, at any stage of development and at any age there can occur abuse, trauma, loss of a magnitude beyond what we are capable of withstanding, bringing a confusion or disorder so severe that further development is brought to a halt. Depression of the severest sort can follow; the loss of what was once a hearty appetite for life. To the individual in this state, the notion that there might be some level of integration at which point the pain is healed and perspective restored seems like a lie the as-yet-unaffected tell themselves.

ADDICTION

And then, complicating things further, there is the problem of addiction... to drugs, alcohol, but also to activities, habits, patterns of escape and avoidance. Let's say that disorientation to some degree enters your life. To address the disorientation, you turn to whatever will offer relief. And for a while it works. Increasingly, however, to find relief, you discover that you must increase the dosage. Opiates, alcohol, shopping, sex, television, prescription medications, gaming, even our work can offer escape and, thus, relief. But in time, if engaged in often enough, each of these escapes can create an appetite that if not fed, results in withdrawal cravings. We find we are engaging in our chosen escape not so much for the pleasure or relief it offers, but because by engaging in it, we avoid the anxiety now associated with its absence.

Trauma, loss, addiction, disorder and disorientation, these must be addressed for development to proceed. Indeed, addressing the disorder in our lives is one of the ways in which development occurs, and one of the ways in which we create readiness for further growth. To address our disorder (or to help others address theirs), whatever form the disorder takes, is to engage in ethical behavior. It is behavior that makes self- and other-destructiveness less likely and the fulfillment of inherent possibilities more likely. This is one of the themes that runs throughout the ethics of human development and, in particular, in what is called the Personal Growth Ethic: *It is ethical to address the developmental requirements of the self, unethical not to do so; ethical to increase the capacity for ethical conduct in self and others, unethical to stop growing as a person—this so that a greater, more inclusive order can evolve, creatively, consciously, with less violence and harm to self and others in the process.*

EASIER TO SAY THAN DO

So much easier to say than do. The full realization of inherent possibilities is an arduous task. There is the addressing of what holds us back (the unasked-for trauma, abuse, loss, perhaps the buildup of the trouble we have given ourselves), and there is the resistance to change, even to the change we say we value. Einstein said that the forces operating in the unfolding universe are fear and longing. So, too, in our individual lives.

With each level in the Five Levels sequence, consciousness expands. Gradually, the individual becomes aware of her own conditioning, aware of the subtle ways in which she is mechanical or robotic, rather than free-flowing and aware. Fear leads us to accept the current "holding pattern" even though it constrains us, pinches us, keeps us partially entranced. On the other side of things, however, is the longing for greater freedom, greater ease with oneself and others. The ability to be relaxed and at home in an ever-widening circle of people, situations, and settings.

INHERENT POSSIBILITY

What, then, is our aim? To love and be loved. To live fully and to the benefit of oneself and others. To be well-functioning *(humming),* ethically creative, in touch with the awe and wonder of life. We should ask: *What does it mean to turn the Fool loose?* It means the ability, increasingly, to live unguardedly, playfully, confident that intentions are pure, confident also that one can create a peaceful, perhaps loving solution should difficult situations arise. It is an achievement of a high order.

> (NOTE: I feel I must offer the following... There are few things more tiresome, boring, or potentially disruptive, even dangerous, than is the *premature release of the fool.* The individual full of self-importance, full of certainty, ready to impose what he does not know on others. The folly of youth, to be tolerated unless it limits or harms others. We are all learning and as we learn, we look back, sometimes embarrassed, sometimes shuddering at the ways in which we were unaware of what we were doing, unconscious and foolish, wondering if we were seen through as our foolishness is so apparent to us now.)

Of the gifts we might give others, the gift that is certain to be a contribution is our embodiment of a fully realized, fully mature self, creatively and ethically involved with the possibilities of the moment (the Fool turned loose with no ill-intent left in him). Respect for the best in others is expressed in this way, as is one's love of life. It is this gift that in the giving offers fulfillment to the giver while stirring awareness and encouraging psychic integration in the individual to whom it is given.

VALUING HUMAN DEVELOPMENT

It is the rare individual who is situated stably at Level V in our schematic. But one of the many things that characterize the conduct of such an individual—or that characterizes Level V conduct whenever we engage in it—is the honoring of all levels in the developmental sequence. That is what characterizes the mature individual: His or her conduct reflects an allegiance to human development overall and, thus, to an honoring of each level as a part of a process that, if not stifled or in some way distorted, serves the expansion of awareness and the flourishing of life as a whole.[5]

To review: At Level I, the individual is driven instinctively by concerns for survival (and necessarily so). At Level II, the focus is on security and acceptance, on readying oneself for membership in family/community/society. Level III champions the right of the individual to stand out, to strengthen the position of the self within existing contexts, and to win and/or acquire territory (of whatever sort), while Level IV addresses the need for rhyme and reason, the need to experience these conditions, to see and create with them in mind. Only with Level V do we integrate all previous motives into a larger framework that recognizes the value of each without allowing any one to be preeminent. Each is seen and honored as a developmental step readying the individual with the capacity to embrace the next step without allowing any step to serve as end point. Indeed, from the vantage point of Level V, there is no end point, though a critical point is reached when development itself—of self and others—is valued and made the focus.

> (NOTE: For a lovely literary expression of this same point, see Norman Spinrad's novel, *Child of Fortune*: *"For while the subject of my sanity at any stage of the tale and the sequence in which my consciousness revolved was to be a matter of endless learned debate by Healers and mages far better versed in the scientific lore than I, in the entirely amateur opinion of the subject in question, my full humanity was restored when I accepted responsibility, however reluctantly, for preserving the humanity of others."*[6])

A BEHAVIORAL VIEW

In the end, it is behavior—choices and the values revealed by those choices—that defines one's level of development. The behavior of those at Level V is characterized, among other things, by the artful inviting out of human potential, the skillful shepherding and shaping of progress on the Yellow Brick Road (though not by shaping and interaction alone but also by example and inspiration). Behavior of this sort, with ends so clearly in service to others, can penetrate defenses (not invariably but with greater likelihood than any other means) and be recognized as friendly to our deepest and most essential nature.

It is true that individuals who exhibit conduct of this sort can unintentionally threaten others with their freedom, their capacity to disregard the conventions that hold others of us in place. Still, the reason in and for their behavior, if glimpsed at all, is disarming. It is natural to be taken with what they model: the freedom to be natural,[7] the playfulness and compassion that spring from the person in love with life. We are drawn to them because they model the realization of our desire to be liberated and whole. They speak to the best that is in us and to what we would have more of if we can find our way to it: enlightenment, adulthood in the fullest sense, realizing that it flowers differently in every individual who achieves it. We can thwart the pull exerted by their example. We can be deeply suspicious of levels of development different from our own. And, for whatever reason, most of us do step off the path before we reach Level V adulthood. Still, the desire for the realization of inherent possibilities remains. Our heads are turned by the beauty we see in others—the behavioral and ethical beauty—and we reach for it, at some level identifying with it, even if we are unable to exhibit it ourselves.

SUMMARY

The opening passage of Part I quoted economist E. F. Schumacher: "If a thing is said to be good but no one can tell me what it is good for, how can I be expected to take any interest in it? If our guide, our annotated Map of Life, cannot show us where The Good is situated and how it can be reached, it is worthless." Part I has been an attempt to address the first part of Schumacher's concern: to show by means of a Map of Life where the Good is situated. It lies, according to the map and overview presented here, in the direction of our development as integrated, free, and enlightened selves, creatively and ethically engaged in furthering—directly or indirectly—that same development in others. In that direction (and in that development) lies The Good... an increasing capacity to engage in conduct that reflects a concern for the wellbeing of oneself and others, and so, for a peaceful, creative, ethical future.

As to the second part of Schumacher's concern ("How can The Good be reached?"), Part II discusses the ethics of human development.

Part II

Human Logic and the
Ethics of Human Development

"The outstanding character of the hyper-organic level (of evolution) is the emergence of selves . . . It is the development or realization of selves that constitutes the 'good' . . . and the theory of ethics that makes this the locus of value is called the ethics of self-realization. By this is meant that the locus of the good is not found in pleasure, nor in organic survival or welfare, but in the complete energizing of our capacities as selves or persons."[1]

—Wilbur Marshall Urban
Fundamentals of Ethics

Economist E. F. Schumacher asks: *How is the Good reached?*

In line with what was presented in Part I, that is the same as asking: *How do we evolve and mature as individuals? How do we realize the constructive fulfillment of our inherent possibilities?* In Urban's phrase, *how do we bring about the complete energizing of our capacities as selves or persons?* The answer, as suggested in the *Preface,* is through conduct in accord with human logic.

THE ETHICS OF HUMAN DEVELOPMENT

The ethics of human development (twelve ethics plus accompanying corollaries) are an attempt to give body and detail to the notion of human logic. Instead of calling them the ethics of human development, they could, as readily, be called the ethics of personal growth, the ethics of personal responsibility, the ethics of teamwork and collaboration, even, to borrow Wilbur Marshall Urban's phrase, the ethics of self-realization.

Before discussing the ethics, a qualification is required. *Trust, integrity, fairness, respect—* terms so often found in ethical codes—are not found for the most part in the ethics of human development. Rather, the attempt here is to detail how one *operates* when behaving with these qualities. Here, the attempt is to leave behind the looseness of those terms and in the process invite a greater degree of both clarity and self-examination.

The qualification is this: The ethics of human development offer a prescription, a recipe— one that aims us in the direction of what is most likely the proper course of action. Still, there are exceptions. Some situations may call for behavior other than the behavior prescribed by the code. In those cases, our allegiance must be to the moment, the situation at hand, and not to the code. The expert chef follows the recipe to a T unless knowledge or intuition suggests that by varying the recipe a more perfect dish can be created. The ethics of human development point us in the direction most likely to serve the cause of human development but may not serve that cause depending on the variables at play.

It is worth pointing out, however, that our ability to discern and make exceptions to the code improves with advancing development. Too often, we make exceptions not because the situation calls for it but because we are afraid to proceed. As development advances, fear less often rules the day, and the honoring of oneself and others, regardless of fear or momentary difficulty, increasingly wins out (this being one measure of personal development).

So, to reiterate, the ethics of human development are an attempt to give body and detail to the notion of human logic, to operationalize the concept. The fundamental value to which the ethics are anchored is human development (and all that is implied by that phrase: creativity, courage, compassion, the mature mind of Level V). And while many variables come into play in any given situation (gender, race, class, ethnicity, etc.)—variables that may call for exceptions and/or differences in style or expression—the code remains relevant because the attempt here is to reach past those differences to the humanity we have in common.

What follows are the twelve ethics of human development. Following the statement and explanation of each ethic or corollary are quotes from various sources and, in several cases, comments from participants in ethics of human development workshops.

The first ethic to be considered is the Organizational Ethic. This ethic focuses on our life in organizations, primarily the workplace. The other ethics are then added, never leaving the workplace or organizations in general but gradually expanding the sense of what is meant by organization to the full range of everyday life.

> Finally, I feel compelled to offer the following: The detailing of the twelve ethics of human development can be dry reading. My hope is that the quotes from other sources and the comments from workshop participants will enliven the text. However, if you believe you grasp the meaning of each ethic and corollary and are in no need of the rationale that is provided, then skip forward as you wish. The justification and human logic of each ethic is there, if needed. I do not want to bore you, dear reader. I want to communicate the behavioral, psychological, and developmental importance of each ethic as best I can. Their relevance, I believe, critical to our wellbeing as individuals and as a society.

"Here, in this poor, hampered, despicable Actual,
wherein even now thou standest, here or nowhere
is thy Ideal: work it out Therefrom."

Zeno quoted in *Marcus Aurelius*
—Henry Dwight Sedgwick

". . . This is the final meaning of work: the
extension of human consciousness."

—D. H. Lawrence

The Organizational Ethic

It is ethical to serve, refine, and advance the organization you have chosen to join. It is unethical to harm it.

If we feel we have chosen for ourselves the organization of which we are a part, that we have come to it voluntarily and that it is worthy of our involvement, then our task is to serve it, refine it, advance it to the best of our ability. Our task is to help it find and realize its potential. In so doing, we discover that we must find, express, and perhaps expand our own potential. We must, for example, acquire new skills, refine and practice existing skills, overcome our disinclination to do either, assume responsibility for outcomes, manage our energy and our attitude. By this ethic we serve the development of both organization and self. Each is advanced by our effort.

On the other hand, to harm the organization, its prospects for survival and long-term success, is to harm ourselves, since our success—other things being equal—is bound up with the success of the organization.

Beyond that, however, should the organization not succeed despite our best efforts to serve it, we will have benefited nevertheless since by our efforts we will have kept our capacity to contribute exercised. We will have kept ourselves ready and in practice should we choose to join another organization. So, in more than one way, we harm ourselves by not attempting to serve, refine, and advance the organization of which we are a part. On the one hand, our prospects for success, wrapped up as they are with the success of the organization, diminish as the organization falters and, on the other hand, our capacity to serve and contribute weakens as we fail to exercise it.

There are ten corollaries that accompany Ethic 1. Together they help define what it means to serve, refine, and advance the organization we have chosen to join.

Corollary 1:
It is ethical to learn everything you can about the organization of which you are a part, its purpose, the vision that guides it, its rules, practices, procedures, its parts and how they are connected, its history and status. It is unethical to remain organizationally ignorant.

The more we know about the organization of which we are a part (i.e., its strengths and weaknesses, the direction in which it wishes to grow, etc.), the more likely we are to know its needs. This puts us in a position to help it, to innovate to its advantage.

Further, the more we know about the organization, the less likely we are to undermine it unknowingly, i.e., the less likely we are to make changes in one part of the organization that have undesired consequences in other parts of the organization. In other words, the more we know about the organization, the more able we are to consider the whole when deciding to act in any one section or part.

Finally, the more we know about the organization (what it stands for, what it is seeking to accomplish, etc.), the more likely we are to recognize offers, proposals, and courses of action that represent conflicts of interest. The sooner a potential conflict of interest is detected, the easier it is to avoid or correct. This helps to spare all involved from problems that can have serious legal, ethical, and financial implications.

All this being said, we obviously cannot know everything about the organization(s) of which we are a part. There is often too much complexity. But we can continue to learn, discover, and deepen our knowledge, with particular focus on the organization's goals, practices, and products. The spirit of Corollary 1 is this: *Learn everything you can about your organization and continue to learn—with special emphasis on the essentials—lest you wake up later in life to the realization that you have been serving something you do not believe in.* For your own wellbeing, it is important that you serve an organization whose purpose and means are acceptable to you, whose ethics and values are consistent with your own. It is important that you feel your life being well used through affiliations established because you believe in them. It is dishonoring to yourself and to those with whom you are involved to do otherwise.

> "… be guided by this rule: An employee cannot have
> too much information."
>
> —James A. Autry
> The Meredith Corporation

Corollary 2:
It is ethical to learn about the needs of those served by your organization (i.e., who they are and what they value), ethical also to learn about the needs of those within the organization served by your division or part. It is unethical to remain ignorant of the needs of those you serve, whether customers, consumers, clients, students, or fellow employees.

Ultimately, the survival of any organization depends on its ability to meet the needs of those it serves. If their needs are not met, they will go elsewhere, dropping their affiliation and no longer contributing their resources—in whatever form—to the organization. An organization cannot sustain itself without the support of those it intends to serve.

Of course, the degree to which an organization can meet the needs of those it serves depends to a considerable extent on the degree to which individuals within the organization meet the work and performance needs of one another. Thus, each member of the organization must strive to meet the work needs of internal consumers/customers/workmates/etc. By meeting those needs, internal kinks are removed, and organizational performance improves.

Thus, the more we know about those we serve, whether inside or outside the organization, the more productively creative we can be. Our knowledge of their needs puts us in a position to refine existing products, practices, procedures, and to invent new ones. This increases the organization's value to those it serves and so, its likelihood of survival and success.

Behind this corollary is the notion discussed briefly in the *Preface:* We serve ourselves when we serve others (i.e., the gift is to the giver). By serving others, whether they are inside or outside the organization, we not only increase our value to them and to the organization, but we also feel the satisfaction that comes from effectively serving others.

"Renewal comes through genuine service to others."

—Max DePree
Chairman and CEO, Herman Miller, Inc.

Corollary 3:
It is ethical to perform your role (i.e., your job or duty) accurately, efficiently, and pleasantly. It is unethical not to do your job to the best of your ability.

Inaccuracy, inefficiency, and rudeness all mean more errors in performance and, thus, greater variation in the quality of products and services. This variation and decline in quality threaten organizational success. Add to this the fact that where inaccuracy, inefficiency, and rudeness go unchecked, stress and frustration mount. The organization becomes a less appealing place for both its members/employees and its customers/consumers.

Take but one example: The individual who keeps work away by bristling whenever approached. Managers and supervisors may begin to avoid this individual. This avoidance builds inefficiencies into the organization, as well as resentments as others find they must carry more than their fair share. Or as they notice the distasteful attitude spreading. At base, rudeness and unpleasantness undermine organizational effectiveness (see the next corollary).

It is important to note that organizations hire us or otherwise invite us to join to do a job or fulfill a role. The expectation is that the job will be performed to the best of our ability (i.e., among other things, accurately, efficiently, pleasantly). To fail to so perform is to break the trust, violating the assumption and expectation of a fair exchange.

Finally, it is only by performing to the best of our ability that we can know and perhaps expand our ability. To go through the motions, to coast or "phone in" our performance, is to allow our abilities to deteriorate, our muscles to atrophy. Our best will not be available when we need it, a fact that we, as well as others, will notice. The result, though perhaps gradual, is a loss of self-esteem as we witness our willingness to settle for less than we can give.

"Nearly half the work force expends only the
minimum effort needed to get by."

—Robert H. Rosen
The Healthy Company

—Participant comment
Ethics of Human Development Training Program

Corollary 4:

It is ethical to perform your role (i.e., your job or duty) in a fashion that does not add to the work, hardship, or distraction of others unnecessarily. It is unethical to make work unnecessarily harder for others.

The more unnecessary work, hardship, and/or distraction we impose on others, the more difficult we make their situation, making it all the harder for them to perform in an accurate, efficient, and pleasant manner. The result is that errors increase, quality varies, and the organization experiences the slowdown that comes from resentment, drift, and stress-related fatigue.

According to those who have been in prison, one rule predominates: *Do your own time!* To do someone else's time (i.e., to make it harder for them to do their time by adding unnecessary work, hardship, or distraction) is to invite repercussions, sometimes of a rather serious sort. It is the same in all organizations. To do someone else's time by adding unnecessary work, hardship, or distraction is to invite resentment and create resistance. The result is a loss of interpersonal effectiveness and, eventually, an increase in interpersonal tension.

At the same time, it is true that we can sometimes be confused about what is and is not necessary. What we believe is unnecessary may in fact be necessary, something we would know if we saw fully how the pieces of the organization fit together. Therefore, it is important to seek from others an understanding of how current tasks and requests fit in, and equally important when making requests of others to relate those requests to legitimate organizational ends. By these practices, organizational awareness expands (Corollary 1), as does our skill at both informing and remaining informed.

This corollary invites us to consider how our neediness or lack of self-awareness can result in an inadvertent, perhaps unconscious, spilling over on to others. Desiring escape from boredom, stress, or anxiety, we find that we seek rescue from others, only to discover (or to be told, or perhaps never be told) that there is or may be an inconsiderateness or selfishness or lack of regard for others in our behavior—that we are allowing our needs to blind us to the needs of others, or to the needs of the organization. That's not to say that the needs we are attempting to address are not legitimate. They no doubt are legitimate. But our decision to address them in this way may be counterproductive, creating hidden costs for both us and the organization.

It's also the case that we can simply be ignorant of the etiquette or manners appropriate to a particular culture of work or play. We may be ignorant of the many ways we can find ourselves walking across the green while others are attempting to putt. Through our lack of awareness, then, or our lack of self-control once we become aware, we may cause hardship, distraction, and/or unnecessary work for others. The result is that things become harder, not easier. More energy is required to accomplish the same or less, instead of the other way around. In the end, whether by ignorance or lack of discipline, organizational capacity is reduced.

So, with this corollary, as with many of the others, the underlying theme: *Expand awareness and with that expanded and expanding awareness, exert more control over your conduct so that you are not unconsciously thwarting your own effectiveness or the effectiveness of others.*

> "'Hassle' means that the people inside the company spend more time
> working on each other than they do making something happen..."

> —Phillip B. Crosby
> *Quality Without Tears*

"I don't see a lot of this. I don't think we have this problem at work."

"Are you kidding! What about the staff kitchen? Who do you think winds up cleaning out the refrigerator and doing the dishes?"

"This issue goes as deep as you want to take it. Resentment. Efficiency. Flexibility. Common courtesy. They're all wrapped up in this corollary. Make work unnecessarily harder and all those concerns come into play."

> —Participant comments
> Ethics of Human Development Training Program

Corollary 5:
It is ethical to speak fairly and honestly of organizational members; to say *about* them what you are willing to say *to* them. The same applies to the organization as a whole. It is unethical to engage in malicious gossip, ridicule, or derisive humor.

Nothing so creates disharmony within an organization as do critical comments made about, but not *to*, the parties in question. The actions that flow from these comments—particularly comments grounded in prejudice, anger, or fear—can be extremely destructive not only to those being discussed but to the organization itself. For an individual to discover that he or she is the subject of malicious gossip, ridicule, or derisive humor is for that individual to feel dishonored. It is enough to break the trust necessary for organizational effectiveness. When trust is broken in this way, it is slow to return.

Further, to say *about* others what we will not say *to* them dishonors not only the parties spoken of but also ourselves. At some level, we know or come to know that we are allowing fear, resentment, and/or anger to direct us rather than duty or principle. Instead of seizing our opportunity for personal growth by saying what must be said to the party in question or deciding that it need not be said at all, we fall back into avoidance or denial. We seek individuals with whom to confirm our prejudices rather than choosing to help others, ourselves, and/or the organization evolve.

To be clear, this corollary is not about gossip per se, not about relating informal news within a network of friends and associates. It is about malicious gossip, ill intent. It is not about good-natured teasing or playfulness. It is about ridicule. And it is not about the absence of humor or taking away the opportunity to bond with others through humor. It is about derisiveness, about making others (who would not find it funny) the butt of the joke. In the end, it is about examining our motives and adjusting our speech until they are self-honoring and consistent with the requirements of a culture marked by trust, directness, and candor.

> "…those little differences we have with our fellowmen, insignificant
> disputes, unbecoming conduct…petty gossip…;
> (a man)…should hold them at arm's length…and give
> them (no) place in his reflections."
>
> —Arthur Schopenhauer
> *Counsels and Maxims*

> *"The person caught up in ridicule, gossip, derisive humor… well, that person is in a kind of trance. They may come out of it… maybe… who knows? Something has to wake them up."*
>
> —Participant comment
> Ethics of Human Development Training Program

Corollary 6:

It is ethical to follow the rules, practices, and procedures of the organization. It is unethical to willfully and knowingly violate the rules, practices, and procedures of the organization or to remain ignorant of them.

At the same time, it is naive to think that rules are never to be broken. Therefore, it is ethical to make exceptions to rules, practices, and procedures when such exceptions serve or do not harm the organization. Further, it is ethical to share the reasoning behind these exceptions so that this reasoning can be examined and refined and so that others in the organization can sooner recognize when and where exceptions are appropriate. It is ethical to help others in the organization acquire the discernment that allows them to make exceptions to rules, etc. when such exceptions serve or do not harm the organization.

The rules, practices, and procedures of the organization exist because it is believed or, perhaps, has been found that conduct in accord with them maximizes organizational effectiveness. To willfully and knowingly break the rules, et al, or to disregard them by remaining ignorant of them, is to diminish organizational effectiveness and threaten organizational survival.

When the prescribed rules of an organization are violated and such violations remain a secret, it is impossible to factor such violations into the ongoing effort to account for variations in organizational performance. Or, to put it differently, only by following the prescribed rules of the organization can we judge their adequacy, i.e., whether they effectively steer energy and resources in accord with the organization's mission.

Further, to break the rules that we agreed to follow when joining the organization is to break the trust. When this is discovered, organizations respond by adding policing to ensure compliance. Thus, those who willfully and knowingly break the rules without attempting to correct them (Corollary 7) wind up making the organization more restrictive and so, for many, a less desirable place to be.

That is not to say, however, that rules are never to be broken. As this corollary points out, there are times when breaking a rule either serves or does not harm the organization. However, when these exceptions occur, it is ethical to share the reasoning behind them so that this reasoning can be examined, refined, and perhaps sanctioned. This permits others in the organization to learn when and under what circumstances exceptions may be appropriate.

Finally, the organization's rules etc. indicate how it believes it should operate in the world. By adhering to its rules, we give ourselves the opportunity to see whether the organization is an acceptable, appropriate, even worthy day-to-day fit for us. If it is a good fit, we eliminate by degree the dividedness, if any, we feel about being a part of it. If not a good fit, we put before us, sooner rather than later, critical questions concerning our affiliation and whether we can have the effect, make the difference, or simply be comfortable with ourselves in the way we desire while a part of the organization.

> *"Being on time… that's a real issue for me. Being ready to work when work starts. I know there are things like flextime, four-day workweeks… some jobs can be done from home. That's all fine. But if you're expected to be at a meeting at 3:00, don't traipse in at 3:15."*

> *"On that point, I attended a training event involving an entire orchestra. The whole idea was that orchestras are organizations. Members of the orchestra must make sure their instruments are in tune. They must arrange their seating, the stands holding musical charts, etc. Some come twenty minutes before the start of the performance. Some ten minutes before. But they are ready when the curtain goes up. They come to work in time to begin work on time. I was impressed with that. It was in contrast to what I have seen in a number of organizations (see the Music Paradigm)."*

> —Participant comments
> Ethics of Human Development Training Program

Corollary 7:
It is ethical to seek the correction, modification, and/or revision of rules, practices, and procedures that are inconsistent with the overall purpose and stated values of the organization. It is unethical to accept without seeking to correct organizational practices that harm the ability of the organization to accomplish its purpose.

Corollary 6 requires Corollary 7; they are companion corollaries. For not only are there rules, et al, to which, on occasion, exceptions can be made (Corollary 6), but there are sometimes rules, practices and procedures that are no longer consistent with the mission and stated values of the organization. To go along with such practices without seeking to correct them is to ignore our responsibility to the organization and to ourselves. Rules that do not serve the organization are a waste of time.

Of course, it is possible to be wrong about a rule needing to be changed or a practice needing to be altered. While we may be convinced of the need for a change in this or that rule or practice, others in the organization may disagree and may decide to keep things as they are. Further, because of our exchange with them, we may come to agree, discovering that our view was incomplete and that good reasons exist for leaving things as they are. Or we may remain convinced: The rule or practice is at odds with the best interests of the organization despite what others say. If that is our view, then we are left with a dilemma. Can we accept the compromise imposed by leaving the rule or practice in place? Can we continue to give our full support to the organization? Is further discussion or further action, up to and including leaving the organization, required if the change we feel is so important is not made? Whatever the case, we will be more consciously engaged. By following the requirements of Corollary 7, we will be learning more about the organization (its openness to change, for example). And we will be learning more about ourselves (our ability to present our case, to create solutions, to adapt and change as warranted).

"Set things in order before there is confusion."

—Lao Tsu
Tao Te Ching

"I think it's a good idea to take stock, to periodically ask: What are we doing here? Is our mission what we would have it be? Are our rules and practices consistent with the mission? Are things in order? What needs to be set right? Doing that as an individual is a good idea and doing it as an organization or business or workplace (maybe even a family, as I think of it) is a good idea, as well."

—Participant comment
Ethics of Human Development Training Program

Corollary 8:
It is ethical to create organizational improvements. These improvements may be in the form of or result in increased revenue, decreased costs, improved services, an enhanced organizational culture. But whatever the form or result, it is unethical not to help the organization evolve.

Corollary 8 states that if we have chosen to be a part of the organization, then we must help it evolve. We must do what we can to improve it. Create to its advantage.

Enhance in some way organizational culture... be of benefit to the bottom line... address the structure of the organization, its vision for itself, the way leadership is exercised... make more readable the forms that come across your desk or appear on your screen. The opportunities for improvement in most organizations are everywhere.

An organization that is evolving does not necessarily remain accommodating to all members and consumers. With innovation comes change. However, the likelihood of the organization remaining a good fit for a given member is, in part, a function of that member's ability to meet the requirements of this corollary. Bring about improvements in which you believe and the fit between you and your organization, other things being equal, will improve.

Even if the improvements we attempt to implement are not adopted, and increasingly, the organization does not evolve in the direction that is right for us, we nevertheless serve ourselves by adhering to the requirements of this corollary. Consider the specific ways in which this is so. By our effort, we deepen our knowledge and understanding of the organization and of organizations in general. We learn more about how to work effectively within a network of mixed and competing interests, discovering perhaps how to overcome our resistances, our impedances, increasing our flexibility as we learn to let go and get on with what is relevant. We learn about our current limits, our capacity to do what we say should be done. And we learn that it may be possible to expand our capacity through persistence on behalf of a change in which we believe. It is true that our efforts can result in a more effective and creative organization. But that is only half of it. We also are the benefactor of our efforts—because whether the organization incorporates our improvements, we emerge with a greater capacity to create and thus, with a greater belief in our own ability to establish a beneficial rapport with the world around us whether we stay in the organization or not.

> *"At first, I thought this was a rather strong statement but the more I thought about it… Sure, the organization needs you to contribute but the deeper point is that if you don't find some way to contribute, you're skipping out on yourself, missing an opportunity to stretch and grow. To get in the habit of missing those opportunities, well, you just can't do that. These are the ethics of human development, right?"*
>
> *"I'm glad we're finally talking about creativity. What are we here for, after all. I feel like I'm not myself when I'm not creating, at least not myself in some important way."*
>
> *"You get out equal to what you put in. Isn't that the idea?"*
>
> —Participant comments
> Ethics of Human Development Training Program

Corollary 9:
It is ethical to protect and defend the organization against destructive influences such as outside forces or internal decision-making practices that lead to fraud, libel, or abuse. It is unethical to remain silent in the face of perceived threats to the organization's survival.

The organization that is free of self-destructive activity (fraud, libel, abuse, negligence, theft, etc.) is an organization that is more likely to survive and prosper. Thus, if organizational members speak up (albeit sensitively, discreetly, creatively) as soon as threats to organizational survival are detected, then the organization can steer clear of danger with greater ease and less expense. This means that energy is freed for innovation—energy that would not be available if the organization was mired in legal battles over destructive activity that remained undetected for too long. So, from the organization's point of view, behavior in accord with Corollary 9 is essential to long-term organizational success.

From the individual's point of view, Corollary 9 requires a willingness to address situations that may vary from the uncomfortable to the frightening. To face these situations and behave ethically is a measure of our ability to put fear aside and act on principle. Ethicist John David Garcia expresses this corollary in no uncertain terms: "Never, under any circumstances, knowingly cooperate with or aid any potential client or associate who is engaged in any way in a destructive enterprise. Be uncompromising in this even if it appears that lack of cooperation will lead to economic or physical disaster for you. This last possibility is almost always an illusion, induced by fear." [2]

This corollary, like the previous corollaries, invites us to behave as if we own the organization, as if we are partners in the enterprise, recognizing that our welfare is linked to the welfare of the organization. For the sake of our families, for example, we are hard put to stand by as our organizations (e.g., our workplaces) are weakened by what we believe are illegal or unethical acts. Whistle-blowing is an extreme, and it does have its place. And certainly, society owes much to those who have had the strength to blow the whistle when all other methods failed. However, much trouble, much entrenchment of organizationally destructive activity, can be corrected if individuals speak up as soon as they sense the need to do so. It is our willingness to go along with what we fear may not be in our own best interests, or in the best interests of the organization, that is so damaging.

> "Despite the high rates of sexual assault and harassment — affecting up to 90% of women in some industries — and pervasive discrimination based on race, gender, age, and sexuality — experienced or witnessed by 61% of U.S. employees — reporting rates remain extremely low. A report by the Equal Employment Opportunity Commission found that only 30% of employees experiencing harassment on the basis of gender, race, national origin, disability and other protected classes make internal complaints, and less than 15% file formal legal charges. A meta-analysis similarly found that fewer than one-third of workers even informally talked with a supervisor about the sexual harassment they experienced, and less than 25% filed formal reports with their employers."
>
> *"Do Your Employees Feel Safe Reporting Abuse and Discrimination?" -- Lily Zheng, October of 2020 --* https://hbr.org/2020/10/do-your-employees-feel-safe-reporting-abuse-and-discrimination.

Corollary 10:

It is ethical to leave an organization whose purpose and values conflict with your own. It is unethical to remain in an organization that requires you to violate your values or personal code of ethics.

For our self-respect as well as our health, it is vital that we belong to and serve organizations we believe in, not ones that would have us violate our values or personal code of ethics. The fact that we are serving an organization we do not believe in will not and cannot escape our notice.

Eventually, it will cause our health as well as our self-esteem to suffer.

On the other hand, to serve an organization in which we do believe is empowering. There is a right order and a right livelihood in that arrangement, an alignment with our desire to focus, serve, and create. There are those who may say, "Wait a minute! I can't leave the organization just because by staying I violate my values and personal code of ethics! I've got bills to pay, a family to feed!" And maybe it is true, maybe you cannot leave immediately, for good reason. But you can begin to explore your possibilities and perhaps in the process discover that you can create a way out, doing so responsibly. To work our way out of an undesirable situation and into a desirable one is enormously empowering, undercutting the notion that we are not capable of creating something better for ourselves. It builds a lasting self-esteem, making visible to ourselves and others our unwillingness to settle for a situation that does not fit our need to both contribute and grow.

"Produce what you can believe in."

—Rolf V. Osterberg
"A New Kind of Company with
a New Kind of Thinking" in
The New Paradigm in Business

"If the money is right... well, a person's values can take a back seat. With money, you can buy a lot of good for yourself, and for the people you care about. Maybe you trade a little uneasiness by day for the pleasures of the weekend."

"Is that what this discussion is about? It seems to me we're talking about something much deeper... perhaps the health of your mind and soul. If your affiliations aren't right, I mean, how can you be at home with yourself at the end of the day."

"Soul! Come on! You're going to bring that into the discussion?"

"Why not? I've spent time in jobs I didn't feel good about. You know, get away with whatever you can... That was the spirit of the place. The "bottom line" was all that mattered, no concern for how you treat people. It made me sick."

"I want to say something that hasn't been said. This corollary and the last one... maybe others... It seems to me that we are talking as much about fear as we are about ethics. That's why I don't always behave ethically. I'm afraid of what might happen if I do. I think it's the same for everyone. It's the fear of what might happen if you do report a problem or decide to leave or whatever. I don't think you can talk about ethics without talking about fear, not if you're going to get to the root of the issue."

—Participant comments
Ethics of Human Development Training Program

Ethic 1, the Organizational Ethic, with its ten corollaries, is the most involved of the ethics. Its focus is on our involvement in organizations, the workplace primarily, but not the workplace only. Team, family, etc., as well. We turn now to the remaining ethics. They continue to apply to our organizational involvements, but also, more generally, to our involvement with everyday life.

And lest we lose our theme, we are discussing the ethics of human development. Ethics that serve us, evolve us as we serve others. Even our inability to behave in accord with them—legitimate exceptions aside—is to give ourselves the opportunity for self-review.

"Human beings are perhaps never more frightening than when they are convinced beyond doubt that they are right."

—Sir Lauren van der Post
South African Author

"Piston slap may indeed sound like loose tappets, so to be a good mechanic you have to be constantly attentive to the possibility that you may be mistaken. This is an ethical virtue."

—Matthew B. Crawford
Shop Class as Soulcraft

"To become aware of what is happening, I must pay attention with an open mind. I must set aside my personal prejudices or bias. Prejudiced people see only what fits those prejudices."

—John Heider
The Tao of Leadership

". . . full unfoldment of creativity requires the ending of rigidity."

—David Bohm and F. David Peat
Science, Order, and Creativity

The Open-Mindedness Ethic[3]

It is ethical to be open to the possibility that your view is incomplete, capable of expansion and improvement. It is unethical to ignore information that could allow you and your organization to grow.

The Open-Mindedness Ethic embraces the notion that openness to input, to other views, to novelty, is essential for growth, whether personal or organizational. It requires that we remain curious about life, about how we might perform our duties to ourselves and others more effectively. At base, it is about the cost to oneself when awareness ceases to expand and, instead, hardens or calcifies.

> NOTE: Ethic 2 has as its companion Ethic 3, the Deliberate Action Ethic. Though considered separately, one without the other is incomplete.

The Open-Mindedness Ethic acknowledges the partialness of all views.[4] No one knows the whole story. All views are incomplete. Thus, Ethic 2 requires that we temper our certainty with some degree of doubt so that there can remain reason for experimentation, for acquiring new experience, for considering alternative or novel formulations. It is with this ethic that we counter the rigidity of mind that is the enemy of—the exact opposite of—creative thought and creative work. The Open-Mindedness Ethic attempts to ensure that leeway and play remain in the system so that the system, whether self or organization, may continue to evolve.

In practical terms, this means a willingness to consider the input we receive from others. This does not mean that we act on all the input we receive—only that we are open to it. Of course, there will be many instances when time does not permit the consideration of other views, and we must decide right now in accord with how we see things currently (Ethic 3). But until that time (and immediately after that time), Ethic 2 and the openness it requires define the appropriate stance.

The two corollaries that follow may not rise to the level of corollaries. They are here because they elaborate points made above and because they offer guidance concerning the further implementation and value of Ethic 2. When the time to act has not yet come, when there remains time for the gathering of information, time to work with others on the creation of an environment that supports the creative advance of those within it, then the following two corollaries offer guidance.

> **Corollary 1:**
> **When seeking a larger, more complete formulation or a difficult-to-find solution, it is helpful to ask others what they think. But it is also helpful to precede statements of presumed fact with phrases that leave open the possibility that you may not be right. "As I see it now," "I may be wrong, but it looks to me as if," "My experience in these matters leads me to**

conclude . . ." all are phrases that support creative discourse. They qualify the finality of whatever follows and leave room for creative problem solving (although this may or may not come). It is unethical to speak so as to deny creative input from others.

How we speak to one another influences our willingness to share ideas. To speak as though we are certain of our position can discourage others from sharing their own differing views, at least in a noncombative way. Within most organizations, absolute certainty (e.g., "This is the way it is!" "Case closed!") can lead to withdrawal or resentment on the part of others. On the other hand, to speak in a way that reflects openness invites others to put forward their ideas. This creates a context within which it is easier to find and/or create solutions.

(NOTE: The style of speaking or interacting that invites others to share the best of what they know and are may vary from the one suggested here. With trust, individuals evolve ways of interacting that on the surface might not appear to invite creative exchange—styles that may be dressed in certainty and posturing. But for the individuals involved, they are styles that heighten the creative process, or that cut short formality. These are the creative, playful, even theatrical interaction styles of longtime friends or colleagues. In the absence of such relationships, however, or when in doubt, the straightforward openness and invitation of input called for by this corollary represent the fallback position.)

The point of this ethic (and its accompanying corollaries) is that without some openness, without some doubt concerning the certainty of our position, knowledge cannot advance. Science, for example, proceeds on the assumption that what we know is partial and incomplete. New information can lead to a revision of our view, to its enlargement or advance. In this way, with some degree of uncertainty, our understanding of the world and ourselves expands. Openness to new information is the key—openness to the possibility that our view is incomplete and might be in error.

> "If we are open only to discoveries which will accord with what we know
> already, we may as well stay shut."
>
> —Alan Watts
> British writer/philosopher

"This is fairly basic stuff, don't you think? Invite others to share their views. Listen and be open."

"Yes, basic stuff. That's why it can be so frustrating when it is absent. And angering. I, for one, withdraw. Who needs it? When someone is closed-off, won't listen, dismissive... You would think it's basic stuff, but it throws you when it's not there."

> —Participant comments
> Ethics of Human Development Training Program

Corollary 2:

It is ethical to be open to the possibility that you yourself, or some unknown factor, may be responsible—however minutely—for the undesirable events or outcomes that come your way. It is unethical to presume absolute certainty about the factors motivating personal or organizational behavior. Such absolute certainty can obscure or cut short the examination of other relevant factors and lead to destructive action against individuals rather than to one's growth as a person.

By leaving open the possibility that it might be us or other factors, and not the other person, who is truly and totally at fault, we force an examination of our own behavior. Instead of closing the issue by affixing blame, we explore ways in which we might increase our effectiveness and perhaps our wholeness. By this corollary, we are encouraged to look for and eliminate our blind spots, recognizing that on occasion we ourselves produce the undesirable events that come our way.

Further, by focusing some part of our energy and analysis on ourselves rather than laboring to affix blame, we increase the likelihood that changes benefiting us, and our organizations will follow. Encountering the same problem—to the extent that it is due to previously unidentified or perhaps unconscious factors—becomes less likely as we change what we are doing, no longer behaving in ways that invite the problem or make us vulnerable to it. Actions against individuals may be necessary. Specific individuals may be sufficiently responsible for some undesirable or damaging event. If so, then the proper sanctioning will need to occur. But by following the guidance of this corollary, we increase the likelihood that we will not miss the opportunity to make improvements in ourselves should such improvements be warranted.

> "To become aware of what is happening, I must pay attention with
> an open mind. I must set aside my personal prejudices or bias.
> Prejudiced people see only what fits those prejudices."

> —John Heider
> *The Tao of Leadership*

". . . only deliberate action . . . is distinctively moral."

> —John Dewey
> American Philosopher
> *Morals and Conduct*

"As I said to you when you were going away, take care also of his brother Apollodorus. [He] causes me anxiety when he does what he does not mean to do."

> —Epicurus
> Greek Philosopher
> Third Century BC
> *Fragments*

"The first thing to do in life is to do with purpose what one proposes to do."

> —Pablo Casals
> Cellist

The Deliberate Action Ethic

It is ethical to choose consciously and execute deliberately specific actions that you believe represent the best of your discernible options. When the time to act has come, it is unethical to not do something.

Ethic 3 is the companion to Ethic 2. Each is incomplete without the other. For however desirable and appropriate the openness of Ethic 2, the time to act does come. And when it comes, it is to the requirements of the act that we must turn (even though our view is incomplete). Of course, each of us is left with deciding when the time to act has come and left also with choosing what to do if the time is now.[5] Therein lies our dilemma, and our freedom.

Ethic 3 acknowledges and emphasizes our responsibility to ourselves and to others when it states that when the time to act has come, we must choose to do something.[6] We must make a conscious decision and proceed (even if that decision is to withdraw rather than intervene, in a sense to do nothing). To fail to act is to stand by idly when the opportunity for personal growth presents itself. We are made in such moments (a topic to be discussed in more detail in Part III); or, rather, we make ourselves in such moments, and we make the organizations of which we are a part. What we choose to do when the time to act comes is everything—or leads to everything— and so, our choices must be increasingly conscious. Ethic 3, which on the surface seems so obvious, is an acknowledgment and honoring of our role as agents in the creation of our organizations, our society, and ourselves.

In everyday life, the actual play of Ethics 2 and 3 and the requirements they impose is such that one ethic may never operate in the total absence of the other. While acting (Ethic 3), there remains openness to new information, and this new information may influence the next decision, the next action. This, no doubt, is how it is and how it must be to maximize the transaction between self and world. Emergencies do arise, requiring a focus and concentration that leave little awareness for anything other than the essentials of the act itself. The policeman, the fireman, the surgeon, the soldier, the parent... all find themselves in situations that call for concentrated, immediate action, for decisions that must be based on what has been learned up to that very moment. At the same time, it is to our advantage, and to the advantage of those who will be affected by what we do, to remain as open as possible, as conscious as possible, as sensitive as possible, throughout the execution of the act (that is, throughout the long chain of behaviors that may constitute the act) so that our decision-making can reflect the latest turn of events. In this way, we make it less likely that we will proceed unconsciously at a time when openness to new information would call for a new or different course of action.

The tendency that this ethic (and its companion, Ethic 2) works to counter is the tendency to be unconscious, to become habit- and/or rule-governed, to turn everyday life over to the robot-self. The presumption of Ethic 3 is that we are consciously deciding our way forward, piloting and navigating as opposed to simply and unconsciously living out the dictates of past conditioning.

Augusto Boal, the Brazilian theatrical scholar, writes about how we can allow "the repetitive acts of daily life" to put us to sleep—how we can "perform the play of breakfast, the scene of going to work, the act of working, the epilogue of supper, the epic of Sunday lunch with the family, etc., like actors in a long run of a successful show, repeating the same lines to the same partners, executing the same movements, at the same times, thousands of times over. Life . . . [becoming] a series of mechanizations, as rigid and as lifeless as the movements of a machine."[7] The result is that we can become sleepwalkers, unmotivated by and unable to act on the requirements of our own development—unmotivated, period. When in this condition, we are on hold, hypnotized, closed to the requirements and possibilities of the moment.

On the other hand, to be open to the requirements and possibilities of the moment, whatever they are (the needs/requirements of the body, of others, of the organization, of our own creative callings) and in response to execute the best of our discernible options, is to make ourselves present and engaged. That is ethical. To not act when, clearly, the time to act has come is unethical. And the sad fact is that often the time to act is long overdue and still we have not acted, preferring sleep, hypnosis, the state of being on hold, to the challenge of our own development.

Ethics 2 and 3 call for a life stance characterized by openness and, when the time to act has come, by decisiveness; a stance characterized by the conscious choosing and executing of the best of what we know to do. It is a stance in service to the creative development of ourselves as persons. It is not all that is required of us, and it is not easy, but only by means of this stance do we remain self-directing and, thus, in a position to learn from our experience while thoughtfully and deliberately adding to it.

> "…to get at meaning we must interrupt the habits that structure our daily practice, habits that are crusts that separate us from . . . the springs of meaning-making."
>
> —Bruce Wilshire
> *The Much-at-Once*

"But how do you know when the time to act has come? That might be clear with respect to some issues but not others. Seems like it could vary from person to person."

"I think you know when the time has come. At some point, it becomes clear. And the issue is: do you act or do you put it off, talk yourself out of it, avoid it in some way."

"There's another issue. I think it's relevant. T. S. Eliot said that the problem with most people is that they are 'distracted from distraction by distraction.' I think there is truth in that. Maybe it's a bit harsh. I don't know. But to proceed in accord with this ethic is to willfully cut down on distractions, to focus. Right? To stop side-tracking yourself and get on with things."

—Participant comment
Ethics of Human Development Training Program

"... everything has a tendency to deteriorate. One of the important things leaders need to learn is to recognize the signals of impending deterioration."

—Max DePree
Leadership Is an Art

". . . no system can operate humanely without adequate feedback."

—Philip Slater
Earthwalk

"A man cannot speak but he judges himself . . . Every opinion reacts on him who utters it."

—Ralph Waldo Emerson
American Philosopher
Compensation

The Feedback Ethic[8]

It is ethical to request, encourage, and deliver feedback. It is unethical to ignore or discourage feedback.

Only with feedback are we able to develop, learn, self-correct, self-regulate. Only with feedback do we know if we are on or off course. The Feedback Ethic emphasizes our duty to ourselves and others to make sure that feedback is encouraged, delivered, responded to effectively, so that development occurs, and desired ends are reached.

Perhaps nothing so characterizes the mature adult as does the ability to give and receive feedback. It is nearly an art form. To give feedback in a fashion that is authentic, without diminishment or blame, tailored to the individual and inviting of his or her development, is a notable skill. And just as notable is the ability to accept feedback, to invite it, and then, when it arrives, to respond constructively, turning the feedback, however it is delivered, to the advantage of oneself and others.

Philosopher John David Garcia writes: "The essential thing in any game is to have a strategy that enables us to learn from our mistakes as well as from our successes. When this is the case, we cannot help but improve our strategies every time we play the game. Self-improving strategies are only possible when there is feedback."[9]

For Garcia, to fully utilize feedback, we must put aside fear and defensiveness. Truth must be valued over happiness, and personal development and the development of others valued over things as they are. Only then can the information contained in the feedback be used to full advantage.

The following corollaries expand Ethic 4 into its component themes. Two of the corollaries make specific reference to the use of feedback within the workplace. However, as the text attempts to make clear, they are not limited to that setting.

Corollary 1:
It is ethical to request and encourage feedback on your performance, product(s), and materials from individuals with whom you interact and/or who, in one way or another, receive your services, whether they are inside or outside the organization. It is unethical to ignore or discourage feedback.

If we are interested in whether we are doing right by those we serve, then their feedback will enlighten us. It will let us know, from their point of view, if we are on or off course.

In addition, requesting and encouraging feedback from those we serve, expresses respect. It announces that their opinions matter to us. Responding constructively to the feedback we receive also engenders respect. Those providing the feedback see that the person or organization with which they are dealing is open to change.

Similarly, to respond constructively to the feedback we receive from friends and loved ones is to announce that their opinions matter, and that we matter to ourselves as well—so much so that we will change if there are benefits to doing so. This is self- and other-respecting, and it invites respect. It models a standard that reflects a commitment to personal growth and makes clear that living up to such a standard is doable.

This corollary does not imply that we must act on the feedback we receive. The feedback we receive may not be useful. It does imply, however, that we are open to and welcoming of feedback and that we will not ignore or discourage it when it is offered. While the feedback we receive may not be helpful this time, the feedback we receive next time may be extremely helpful. However, if we have ignored, discouraged, or in some way punished the person from whom we are receiving feedback, then we reduce the likelihood of a next time. Thus, it is self- and organizationally destructive to ignore or discourage feedback, healthy to invite feedback, to be open and alert to what it might offer.[10]

> *"That's what this corollary is about . . . I get it. Asking your customers, your employees, your spouse for their ideas for improving things. No big deal. Easy enough. Until they come back asking for the impossible!"*
>
> —Participant comment
> Ethics of Human Development Training Program

Corollary 2:
It is ethical to offer feedback to those from whom you receive services. It is ethical to acknowledge outstanding performance, just as it is ethical to provide feedback to those whose performance or service threatens the optimal performance of you or your organization. In both cases, it may be unethical not to do so.

Corollary 1 emphasizes the importance of inviting and encouraging feedback. Corollary 2 emphasizes the importance of *giving* feedback. By giving feedback, we provide information others may find useful in their effort to fine-tune their performance or achieve their desired ends.

Acknowledging outstanding performance, for example, or the next advance over past performance (as in the arts of teaching, parenting, and team building), is the hallmark of a positive culture. In such a culture, talent flourishes. Individuals experience support for what they do well (or are attempting to do well) and, increasingly, they are in touch with their desire to realize their potential. They feel safer and more empowered than they otherwise would because they are in a culture interested in seeing and acknowledging the best of what they have to offer.

When given correctly (as discussed in more detail in Corollary 3), feedback requires a concern for the other person while, at the same time, maintaining an allegiance to one's principles. This is particularly true for critical or negative feedback. Individuals who can deliver negative feedback are invaluable to their organizations because they do not compound problems as they work to correct them. They give feedback in a way that makes the recipient's excuse to blame the messenger less likely; more likely to consider the relevance of what is being said. Feedback delivered in this way is a service to the individual and to the organization and, coincidently, serves as a measure of one's own growth. To deliver feedback sensitively, creatively, while remaining true to the mission of the organization and to one's own standards and principles, is to give evidence of one's own capacity to stay on course even in the face of potentially uncomfortable exchanges.[11]

Finally, it is possible in organizations (whether two-person organizations or larger) to feel unseen or unheard. Corollaries 1 and 2 make this condition increasingly unlikely because they encourage a give-and-take on matters relevant to organizational health. The sense of isolation, the sense of not being connected or meaningfully involved, are obviated by these corollaries since they call on us to take responsibility for our own sense of involvement.

Corollary 1: *Invite connection by inviting feedback. Announce thereby your presence in the organization—i.e., your willingness to be critiqued, your respect for the opinion of others, your desire to be connected.* Corollary 2: *Give feedback to others. Confirm their efforts, offer advice (if it seems appropriate to do so), establish connections by speaking to matters relevant to the organization. Also, speak up if feedback is not coming your way. Give feedback on the absence of feedback to avoid colluding silently with the absence of a practice essential to personal and organizational effectiveness.*

If, after all our efforts (in accord with Corollaries 1 and 2), feedback and a sense of connection are still not forthcoming, then that is feedback of another sort: Feedback that casts doubt on the worthiness of the organization and our affiliation with it. Or (and this must always be a consideration) it is feedback on the skill with which we request and offer feedback. It is always possible that our manner, our way of asking for and offering feedback, is threatening, insincere, blaming, and/or not constructive or truly welcoming. Hence, the need for Corollary 3.

> *"What about the other side of it... positive feedback, acknowledging improved or outstanding performance? That takes some skill, as well. Also, it takes a willingness to provide that kind of feedback. I've seen coaches, heck, I've had coaches who never gave any positive feedback. That may work with some players, but it never worked with me. The spirit freezes if criticism is all you hear, and it withers on the vine without the nourishment of positive support."*
>
> —Participant comment
> Ethics of Human Development Training Program

Corollary 3:
It is ethical to deliver feedback sensitively and to accept it graciously. It is unethical to diminish the person to whom you are giving feedback or to punish the person from whom you are receiving it.

"A man cannot speak but he judges himself. Every opinion reacts on him who utters it." (Emerson) For this reason, it is important to give feedback sensitively and to accept it graciously, realizing—

as Garcia points out—that the feedback we give may be more about us than the other person, while the feedback we receive may be correct.

Further, to diminish those to whom we give feedback or to punish those from whom we receive it is self-destructive. In the first instance, the feedback we give will not be heard since the individual is likely to focus on the diminishment and not on the content of the feedback. And in the second instance, the person from whom we are receiving the feedback is less likely to offer feedback in the future if the current effort to do so is punished. Such practices are likely to make the culture of the organization or the relationship between two people increasingly hostile. Only individuals committed to their own growth can rise above this hostility, if it does develop, and continue to give and receive feedback constructively regardless of how the feedback was delivered to them or received by others.

> (NOTE: Again, as indicated earlier, familiarity and fondness can lead to idiosyncratic, tailored, even theatrical or playful modes of exchanging feedback. To the outside observer, these modes may seem insensitive. But the feedback is heard and the obligation to give feedback is not avoided. No affront is taken. An established relationship can permit kindness or regard for the other person to shine through an unorthodox delivery. There is sensitivity and grace in this, as well as love, even though the style departs from what is recommended here. When in doubt, however, when there is not the bond or familiarity or trust, the more formal and careful delivery of feedback, along with the more obviously gracious acceptance of it, is the preferred mode. With this mode, the trust, fondness, and respect so essential to the richness that is interpersonal and organizational life can evolve.)

Finally, the work of Robert Kegan and Lisa Laskow Lahey is instructive with respect to the delivery of feedback.[12] Kegan and Lahey investigated what they called the "language of ongoing regard" and offered the following instruction: When offering feedback, "be direct, be specific, and be nonattributive." Don't dissipate the impact of your feedback by being indirect. Speak directly to the person to whom you are giving feedback and be specific about what it is that has caused you to offer the feedback. Avoid characterization, the ascribing of attributes. The person to whom you are giving feedback knows (or feels she knows) how wonderful (or generous or kind or angry or peaceful) she is. For you to say that she is so wonderful invites her to assess herself and say (to herself, if not to you): "No, I am not really so wonderful (or angry or generous)." By ascribing an attribute, we define the person. And the person, who knows herself better than we do, reacts by deciding how correct we are. If, instead, we share our experience with the person—what she leads us to experience—we take away the inclination to judge us right or wrong. After all, it is our experience. How could we be wrong? This provides what Kegan and Lahey call "a precious kind of information," information on the individual's impact on the world, information the individual can use to define herself.[13]

> *"There's another thing. Tell me I'm wrong if you think I am. Sometimes the feedback we receive is not about some specific skill we're trying to improve.*

Sometimes it's about who we are as a person, at least in that moment. It's about when we're sometimes a jerk, or rude... how we're taking it out on others. That's pretty important feedback, don't you think? You may not like to hear it. But you should count yourself lucky if you've got someone who will call you on it."

—Participant comment
Ethics of Human Development Training Program

"So I went to studying it out. I says to myself, I reckon a body that ups and tells the truth when he is in a tight place is taking considerable many resks, though I ain't had no experience, and can't say for certain; but it looks so to me, anyway; and yet here's a case where I'm blest if it don't look to me like the truth is better and actually SAFER than a lie. I must lay it by in my mind, and think it over some time or other, it's so kind of strange and unregular. I never seen nothing like it."

—Mark Twain
The Adventures of Huckleberry Finn

". . . most people opt for a life of very limited honesty and openness and relative closedness, hiding themselves and their maps from the world . . . [Those who tell the truth] are not burdened by any need to hide . . . They do not have to construct new lies to hide old ones."

—M. Scott Peck
The Road Less Traveled

". . . my driving conviction is that all humanity is in peril of extinction if each one of us does not dare, now and henceforth, always to tell only the truth and all of the truth, and to do so promptly— right now."

—Buckminster Fuller
Critical Path

The Truth-Telling Ethic

It is ethical to tell the truth, to be honest. Truth-telling promotes clarity and allows you to match resources with greater precision to the demands of the moment. It is unethical to lie. Lying creates misinformation, confusion, and distrust, threatening your ability to survive, adapt, and prosper.

The Truth-Telling Ethic states that it is ethical to tell the truth, to be honest. It goes without saying that here we are talking about the truth as we know it, the truth of our experience, in accord with our own sense of principle and privacy. Obviously, there are certain questions the answers to which are no one's business but our own, as well as comments we could make that would serve only to hurt or damage others. We do not answer some questions, and we do not express some views, however true we may believe them to be, because to do so would serve no purpose but to harm others.

Here, with this ethic as elsewhere with the ethics of human development, there are exceptions. Obviously if by telling the truth we would put someone's life in danger or hurt their feelings unnecessarily, we make an exception. But making exceptions is a tricky business. We should not make exceptions for personal gain or convenience. Only if the individual cannot utilize the truth constructively for personal growth are we justified in withholding it. And making such a judgment requires a discernment of such an exalted degree that only genuine love for the other can drive it. This was M. Scott Peck's point in his book *The Road Less Traveled*, and having made this point he cautions, ". . . in assessing the capacity of another to utilize the truth for personal/spiritual growth, it should be borne in mind that our tendency is generally to underestimate rather than overestimate this capacity."[14]

Ethic 5 addresses the disabling effect of contradiction; the effect of saying one thing to one person and something else to another person; of espousing publicly what we do not believe privately; of saying one thing and doing another. The assumption operating here is that psychological integration is an inherent drive. Within our bodies, our psyches, our families, even perhaps within the human family, we do not wish to be a house divided. We desire integration, and truth-telling supports this integration, lying does not. Lying creates contradiction or is the result of unresolved contradictions, and these contradictions require energy to sustain—energy that instead could be used for constructive purposes.

Will Schutz, one of the founders of the human potential movement, offered the following:

> "Honesty and openness are the keys to your evolutionary growth. Being honest allows your bodymind to become a clear channel for taking in all the energy of the universe, both inside and outside your body, and to use it profitably. You must

spend great amounts of energy to hide your feelings, thoughts, or wishes from other people, and even more energy to keep them from yourself. To withhold secrets requires a tightened body; it requires vigilance, shallow breathing, physical exertion and a preoccupation with your own safety. This results in your missing all sorts of stimuli because your bodymind is not relaxed enough to allow them in."[15]

When we lie, we must keep track of what we said. Otherwise, we run the risk of being found out. This means that the memory and mental capacity that we otherwise would have available are devoted instead to keeping things straight. On the other hand, to tell the truth, one's own truth, without compromise, but with the open-mindedness of Ethic 2, is to serve the cause of clarity. Perspective is furthered. As Schutz points out, truth-telling or honesty helps ensure "a clear channel for taking in all the energy of the universe," a bodymind less cluttered, less noisy, less divided, and thus more present and available to the creative opportunities of the moment. At base, truth-telling announces the individual's interest not in manipulating others, not in hiding or self-protection, but in personal growth.

For this reason, the decision to abide by the Truth-Telling Ethic is one of the most important decisions we ever make. It is the decision to embrace life as it is, not as we would embellish it; a decision to accept what experience and current reasoning tells us is so and thus, a decision not to perpetuate the party line however convenient or self-serving it would be to do so.

This, of course, must be accompanied by the openness and humility of Ethic 2. Our own personal truth is not the whole truth, and perhaps not the truth at all but rather the latest and best report we can offer on what is happening to us—the truth as we know it now. Still, with this step, the hiding is over. Instead, there is an individual secure enough and committed enough to submit his development to a principle, believing that a shorter, more direct route to understanding exists, a route that calls for the voicing of one's truth in situations that matter, withholding it—if at all—out of regard for the welfare of others.

In organizations, truth-telling and honesty go hand in hand with organizational health. Without truth-telling, without the telling of difficult but necessary truths, the organization and its members cannot identify and address their problems. Nor can they build the trust needed for personal and organizational effectiveness. With trust comes possibility. Without trust, all parties find themselves immersed in second-guessing. Of course, there are times within organizations when the truth might need to be withheld. But for those individuals intent on finding exceptions, it is important to remember that when it is learned that the truth has been withheld, the trust that is broken will remain broken unless it can be concluded that genuine concern for the other, and not personal gain, was the motive.[16]

Finally, to lie, to withhold the truth, to break the trust among friends, colleagues, and associates, to so act without justification, is to betray. And betrayal, when discovered, is profoundly shocking, a blow to the solar plexus. When we discover we have been betrayed, we feel outraged. But we also feel dishonored and shamed. And while we can blame the other person for what they have done to us, often (and for the longest time) we may also blame ourselves. It is possible to so internalize our experience of betrayal—depending on its severity and the age at which it occurs—

that it shakes our sense of self-worth for a lifetime. "What is it about me that invites this dishonoring? I must not be worthy." However in error this conclusion, it nevertheless can characterize the inner dialogue of the individual—the child, for example, or the young adult—who turns on themselves as if they were worthy of the betrayal they received.

There is also shame if we are the person who has done the betraying, certainly when the betrayal is discovered, if not before. And there is self-disgust. Whether betrayer or betrayed, we can find our experience "de-spiriting." And one of the dangers is that we will use our experience as an excuse for engaging in more of the same. "It's a dog-eat-dog world. Look out for yourself. It was done to me; I can do it to others. It's part of the game." In this way, an organizational culture unravels and so, too, personal relationships.

Or we can call a stop to the betrayal, taking a stand against our lack of fortitude. We can call a stop to it—and often do—because the pain of a situation lacking truth-telling and honesty is too great. There is no growth in such a situation, no unfolding of inherent possibilities. And that, ultimately, is painful. And while calling a stop to it could prove difficult, perhaps even painful in the short run, it is nevertheless a step in service to one's development as a person. With this step, the individual opts for a bodymind less cluttered and less divided, more the clear channel of which Schutz spoke.

> "…and the law of chivalry demands that I keep my
> word before I satisfy my wishes."
>
> Don Quixote to his squire, Sancho
> —Miguel De Cervantes
> *Don Quixote*

"I think the first thing to say is that words penetrate. They go through you to your muscles and organs. When you discover you have been lied to, it bends you over. You may be standing upright but inside you've had the wind knocked out of you."

"Of course, you can get good at lying just like you get good at anything. But unless you're a sociopath, whatever that means, I think it catches up to you. I don't know how, but I think it does. Maybe, if you continue to get away with your lies, you become cynical. "The world is full of suckers." Some of your humanity slips away."

"I mean, terminal diagnoses… We didn't tell my uncle. What good would it have done? Maybe you think we should have told him and maybe we should have. I don't know. He had his affairs in order. He was happy to be going home. He still had his mobility and a lot of good days. What if it had been a small child? These are hard calls. Maybe we were avoiding a painful moment with our uncle. Maybe you think we were being cowardly. Maybe he had a right to know. He probably did have a right to know. I'm not saying we were right."

> —Participant comments
> Ethics of Human Development Training Program

"Whenever smart and well-intentioned people avoid confronting obstacles, they disempower employees and undermine change."

—John P. Kotter
Leading Change

". . . Everything we shut our eyes to, everything we run away from, everything we deny, denigrate or despise, serves to defeat us in the end. What seems nasty, painful, evil, can become a source of beauty, joy and strength, if faced with an open mind."

—Henry Miller
Twentieth-Century American Writer

The Pain-Directed Ethic

It is ethical in ongoing personal and organizational development to work first on the issue causing the most pain, then to work on the next most painful issue, and so on, in this way creating improvements in the sequence most likely to ensure not only survival but also health and wellbeing. It is unethical to ignore painful issues. By ignoring painful issues, we allow them to compound, threatening all the more the ability of the person or organization to accomplish his or its purpose.

Nothing so retards development as the willingness to escape from and/or avoid difficult and painful issues. When we use such stratagems (escape and avoidance), the painful issues rarely go away. Instead, they worsen, further inclining us toward escape and avoidance until at last, the issue becomes a crisis that must be addressed if we are to avert disaster.

To put it another way, the painful and difficult issues that confront us, whether as individuals or within our organizations, rarely emerge fully blown. For the most part, they start out small and then grow because instead of dealing with them when first noticed, we turn away, only to discover when we turn back days, weeks, or months later that they have compounded and now require far more of us than would have been the case had we dealt with them initially.

The Pain-Directed Ethic attempts to eliminate escape and avoidance from one's management style. It asks us to identify what is not working both in our lives and in our part of our organizations and then calls on us to address the most severe of these—the issue that represents the greatest threat to our ability or our organization's ability to accomplish our/its purpose. And when that issue or problem is resolved, or when all that can be done today has been done, to move to the next most severe problem, and so on. In this way, the entity in question, whether self or organization, is brought with maximum speed to a more smoothly functioning, integrated whole, and kept there.

Leadership is distinguished by this ethic, by its willingness to face issues as they arise rather than putting off the duty to their organization because of fear or inconvenience. Some of the best organizational leaders begin their tenure by asking: *What is the greatest threat to our organization's ability to accomplish its purpose, the issue that is—in that sense—causing the most pain?* And they proceed amidst their other everyday duties to make that item their number one organizational development priority. When that issue has been addressed, or as the plan to address it is underway, the next most serious or painful issue is identified and addressed, and so on, until the issues that must be faced are, on average, smaller and less intractable, and so require less time and energy to address.

(NOTE: As an aside, it is not unreasonable to suggest that the issue causing individuals and organizations the most pain is, in fact, the absence of this ethic—the escape, avoidance, and procrastination of individuals and organizations with respect to the difficult and painful issues that confront them.)

It was this ethic that Gandhi spoke to with his admonition: "Do what is right, now!"—that is, do not procrastinate. Address the painful issue now, before it compounds and becomes more painful still. And it was Lao Tsu, the Taoist philosopher, who expressed the benefit implicit in the embracing of this ethic when he wrote, "Because the sage always confronts difficulties, he never experiences them"[17]—which is to say, he confronts them as soon as they are detected, when they are hardly difficulties at all.

With that said, several additional points concerning this ethic are worth making. First, it is true that some issues in one's life or in organizations have been ignored for so long that they have become mountains, the prospect of scaling them overwhelming. To deal with these issues, a capacity must be developed, perhaps by taking on smaller, less daunting issues until, with success, a greater capacity emerges. This, in fact, may be the way we address the issue—gradually, by approximation.

However, even with this most reasonable of stratagems, we can find that we are avoiding the issue looming before us, an issue that becomes larger with each passing day. Believing that we are building capacity may be the way we trick ourselves into thinking we are addressing the issue when, in fact, it is the clever way we are avoiding it. Clearly, we must work up to some issues, but it is also important to remember that once engaged with what we know we must address, we often find we have more capacity than we had presumed.

Of course—in accordance with Ethic 2—we must be open to the possibility that we may be wrong about the nature of the problem before us. This is always possible. However, only by attempting to deal constructively with what we believe to be the problem do we begin to narrow in on its true nature. We may discover that what we thought was the problem was in fact an outcropping, a symptom, and not the real problem at all, our initial effort serving only to improve our understanding. We are always in danger of misjudgment, of acting in error. And yet, only by proceeding with the requirements of the Pain-Directed Ethic and the ethics of human development in general can we discover the true nature of the problem before us and how best to address it.

Writer / mystic Eckhart Tolle provided an analogy that turns this analysis in the direction of the self. Too often, writes Tolle, "We find abhorrent the image we see reflected in the mirror and so, we attack the mirror."[18] We go after the reflection and not its source. The problem is presumed to be out there, and so long as that is the presumption, the problem will remain. What we see out there can reflect what we are doing or failing to do in our everyday lives, in our treatment of ourselves and others. This happens often enough for there to be value in asking whether by some behavior or stance, the problem we face is self-caused. This question promotes self-examination and can lead to changes in doing and being that are liberating for both self and organization.

Obviously, if there is something wrong in our lives or in our part of our organization, if there is negativity, dysfunction, or pain, then change is required. However, if we are unable to initiate the change, unable to behave in new ways that might bring about the change, continuing to behave as we have in the past even though it has been to no avail, then part of the problem is in us. We are stuck or rigid in ways that conspire to keep things as they are. The Pain-Directed Ethic, by its insistence that painful issues be addressed, leads us on a search for the source of the pain, and sometimes those searches lead back to us.

So, to ignore a pain-producing issue and our role in solving it is unethical not only because it is self- and organizationally destructive but because it ignores what may be an opportunity for personal growth. Pain announces that there is a problem in the system. Some part or parts are suffering while other parts remain unaffected for now. The Pain-Directed Ethic requires that we confront the source of the pain, track it down, resolve it so that the system is no longer under threat. This can lead to a confronting of our fears, our resistances to change; to a confronting of our map of reality—which in turn leads, invariably, to a test of commitment and flexibility.

No matter how challenging the issue, however, when we proceed in accord with the requirements of this ethic, we at least find we are fortified by the relevance of what we are doing. To work on the issue we believe is causing the most pain is to leave no question about the relevance of our effort. To resolve the issue, whatever it is and wherever it lies, is to display mastery over some small part of our world, and mastery over ourselves, as well.

> *"I think it's an impressive person who takes this ethic seriously. If you're going to realize your potential or the potential of your group, then you have to be willing to face the stuff standing in your way. And, yeah, sure, it's often a relationship issue."*

> *"To me, the body is the messenger. Ignore the signals your body is sending you and things get worse. The stress-based headache becomes an ulcer. The heart rate arrhythmia becomes a heart attack. I think this is true whether you're talking about yourself, or the organization as a body (of sorts), even the body politic. Ignore the pain and things get worse."*

> *"We had an example of this in our family. Someone in our family was in a lot of pain. I say "pain", it must have been painful, but not physical pain. More like psychological pain, severe and sad disconnection, I'm not sure but I do know that it was affecting the entire family. No one, however, was doing anything about it. No one was attempting to address it. When the family would get together, the only thing you would hear people say are things like, "Who brought the casserole?" Finally, the situation got worse and worse until it exploded. Maybe no one had the skill to deal with it, but it seems like we could have done more than we did."*

> —Participant comments
> Ethics of Human Development Training Program

"Only mutually voluntary transactions can ever be ethical or creative."

—John David Garcia
Creative Transformation

"Bad faith: Seeking to blame someone or something for what one has done freely oneself . . . pretending that one is born . . . determined . . . instead of recognizing that one spends one's life . . . making oneself."

From Hazel E. Barnes'
Introduction to Jean-Paul
Sartre's *Being and Nothingness*

". . . choice is burdensome and effortful, it requires resolution, a lifting up of the power of personality against the spiritual gravitation of impulse or habit or sloth. Choice is creation, and creation is labor."

—Will Durant
The Story of Philosophy

The Free Choice Ethic

It is ethical to assume that you are choosing to do all that you do, that you come to your tasks by choice, that you are involved voluntarily with the requirements of your life. It is unethical to assume, unless extreme circumstances prevail, that you are being made or forced to do anything.

The Free Choice Ethic goes to the heart of the matter, to choice, to what is meant by the term and to why it is so important. None of the ethics discussed thus far, nor any that will be discussed later, stirs so much discomfort. But without choice, there are no ethics. The entire notion of ethics is predicated on the presumption of choice, on the presumption that we are choosing our way forward, our stories composed largely by the choices we make.

And yet, try telling yourself that you do not actually have to do what you are doing, that no one is forcing you to do it. In response, you may hear from inside yourself an uproar: "I have no choice!" But most of the time this is not true and should not be assumed to be true. You may dislike your options, but choice—the freedom to accept, create, transcend, or leave—must be assumed or the entire concept of ethics is out the door.

Still, the presumption of choice, though essential, is often unwelcome because it addresses and undercuts our propensity to think of ourselves as victims; our propensity to conclude that our misery, our disgruntlement, was inevitable, forced upon us by forces larger than ourselves (and indifferent at that), our situation determined by the hand we were dealt.

In fairness, it can be hard, especially later in life or when things have not gone our way, not to conclude that our biology was our destiny, or that our parents, through their limitations, established our own, launching us on a course from which self-directed departures were largely an illusion. And equally hard at times not to point to class, culture, age, gender, race, or ethnicity as the reasons for our developmental stage, psychologically and spiritually. These are potent and relevant factors. They no doubt affect the range of options available at any point in time. Yet as relevant as they are, and though they must be honored for the uniqueness and diversity they insert into the developmental and evolutionary process, they nevertheless serve only to define the stage whereon we operate, not the outcome. The development of higher character, if it is to occur, remains ours alone, something we create through the conscious effort to do so. The Free Choice Ethic encourages us to abandon the victim paradigm and to see the role that choice plays in shaping both consciousness and conduct, with these other factors, potent as they are, saluted for what they contribute but no longer presumed responsible for what we become.

The presumption of choice, however, along with the presumption of being a self-responsible agent, is tricky because, in truth, the self evolves. We do not start out with sufficient awareness to choose and follow through with those options that serve the cause of our own development. We must develop that capacity; as we do so, choice enters our life by degree. With every developmental step, awareness expands and, with it, the capacity to see options, to choose ever more consciously, and so, to exercise responsibility for what we do and become. That is why the ethics of human development, and this ethic, in particular, are not for children. They are for adults and would-be adults who recognize that with the presumption of choice comes the presumption—necessarily and increasingly—of responsibility.[19]

What we are emerging out of as we develop and mature is a life lived unconsciously, a life directed by the programming of the past. What we enter is a life conscious of that programming, conscious of it in all its subtle and profound aspects and, thus, a life in which choice—anchored to reason, principle, and the requirements of further development rather than robotic compliance— can occur. With expanded (and expanding) awareness we see how in the past we have so often proceeded unconsciously. How our current situation is very possibly related to choices we ourselves have made. We begin to take responsibility for our next steps in life as we see options we did not see before. The ethics of human development emphasize education, feedback, and learning as by those means awareness is expanded. But on a more profound level, the ethics of human development presume choice, our capacity for self-direction as increasingly integral to our way of operating in the world.

So, with this ethic, choice is presumed—increasingly so as we develop. Having said that, consider philosopher Jean-Paul Sartre's notion of "bad faith." Bad faith, in Sartre's philosophy, means "Presuming/pretending/behaving as if what is before us is mandatory when it is, in fact, voluntary."[20]

Here is an all-too-common example. Many of us in our day-to-day work lives, in organizations we have chosen to join and from which we are free to exit, approach our tasks as if someone was making us do them, as though we were being forced to do them. Long after joining the organization, perhaps years later, we walk the halls, enter meetings, undertake work-related duties like captives, pretending that what is before us is mandatory and not voluntary at all. And yet, according to this ethic, we are there by choice, free to exit or in some way modify our experience. To pretend otherwise is disastrous for us and for the organization. It is self-dishonoring, psychologically weakening, and an example of how far we are willing to go to avoid the burden and responsibility implicit in choice—in this case, in choosing to be where we have placed ourselves, or in choosing another way of being there, or in choosing something new.

Which team is more likely to succeed: the team comprised of volunteers, or the team comprised of individuals behaving as if they are required to participate? The team comprised of volunteers has the energy, the lack of dividedness, the clarity of purpose to succeed or at least realize its potential. The team comprised of individuals behaving as if they are required to participate merely gets by . . . perhaps not even that, since a subtle form of sabotage is often present in this type of team culture, as members consciously and unconsciously create excuses for not participating fully.

There are consequences for choosing to participate and for choosing not to participate. There are always consequences. The choice to be a part of a team may or may not be an easy one. But it is our choice, nonetheless. The Free Choice Ethic states that you are free to be part of the team or not as you choose. If you are choosing to be on the team, then acknowledge that fact and choose to be there. That does not mean you will not vigorously challenge team practices that you believe hurt the ability of the team to accomplish its purpose. And it does not mean that you will continue to choose to be on the team if, in your view, it is no longer worthy of your involvement. It merely means that if you are choosing to be on the team then be there fully, totally, doing what it takes (within the bounds of your ethical framework) to make the team a success. On the other hand, if you are choosing not to be on the team, then get off. The exercise of bad faith, the denial of your own capacity to create through choice, is destructive and unethical. It is one way to disempower yourself and, in the process, create work, trouble, and hardship for those around you.

It is true that a more complete analysis of the behavior in question, i.e., of the individual who behaves as if he is being forced to do what he is free not to do, includes the fact that at some level the individual feels unseen, unheard, or in some other way disregarded. And so, he pouts, expressing resentment or anger in subtle and not-so-subtle ways.[21] But to wait to be recognized or embraced by the surrounding culture before behaving in ways that honor one's own development is self-destructive. It places one's dreams and aspirations on hold, allowing the will to atrophy, and does nothing to bring about the culture, team, organization, or self one desires. Even if indifference reigns, even if we remain unseen and ignored, still this ethic tells us we must not pretend we have no choice. Honor yourself and empower yourself by recognizing that you very possibly decided your way into your present situation, a journey of many steps, many choices. And now, if you wish, you can change your situation. You can decide your way out, honorably, ethically, though that, too, may be a journey of many steps, many choices. But do not pretend that the power to affect your situation—or your experience of it—lies solely outside yourself. True, there may be factors outside your control. But the capacity to creatively respond to what is given, to choose the option that is likely to expand your freedom and/or your development as a person... that is yours alone, and increasingly so as you so choose. That is the heart of Ethic 7.

This brings one final point to the surface—or perhaps it is merely a restating of what has been said already. With the presumption of choice and the growing degree of responsibility it implies, there come the most challenging of questions, questions that invite a thoughtful overview, a generous and forgiving self-examination. *Who is responsible for your creativity? Who is responsible for the heart and energy you put into your pursuits? Who is responsible for your morale?* These questions suggest how far we might go in the application of this ethic to our lives. Whatever our answer to these questions, the Free Choice Ethic pushes us to entertain and even embrace, if possible, a responsibility that is nearly freedom itself: freedom of spirit, to be exact. Without adherence to this ethic, we cannot travel the full length of the Yellow Brick Road. We pursue the Mature Mind—as described in Part I—through choice, and its achievement is one of the most inspiring of human accomplishments. It is by means of this ethic, with its insistence on extending the reach of our responsibility, that the ethics of human development become the ethics of self-realization.

A few additional thoughts on this very important and perhaps challenging ethic...

As already stated, the Free Choice Ethic raises a complicated and delicate issue: the presumption of choice. We have and make choices and are free to do so. We are not the victims we sometimes portray ourselves to be.

But is that so: We make choices and are free to do so? It is certainly the case that our histories obviously and dramatically affect the choices we make. It might even be accurate to say that our histories determine the choices we make, a statement that undercuts the notion of free choice altogether. We are not outside the web of cause and effect; we are within it, a part of it, everyone acting in accord with the causes that impinge upon them. Where is the freedom in a system in which actions flow necessarily from what has preceded them?

And yet, our histories are learning histories. We learn from our experience. We learn to observe, to engage in forethought, to think about what will happen if we do this or that. We become conscious. And as we become conscious, options appear. At some point, it seems natural and appropriate to say that we have choices. Appropriate, also, to say that we have responsibility for the choices we make.

Is this illusion? Does the complexity of our learning history prevent us from seeing the determinism that continues to operate? Perhaps. In fact, it may not be possible to dispense with that possibility. However, what is presumed here is this: To develop and mature in the Five Levels sense is to experience a shift in the locus of control from past conditioning to a conscious, deliberative, aware self... a gradual shift brought about by the consequences of past acts, consequences that encourage us to pay attention, to think for ourselves, to consider the likely consequences of future acts. We learn to pause, to reflect, to interrupt what were previously automatic chains of behavior with decisions to proceed or not to proceed. And with those learned skills, we become self-directing. We hold ourselves responsible for the choices we make, insisting that we learn from our mistakes—insisting, as well, that ethic, principle, goal, or vision govern our choices, not the restraints of past conditioning.

There are victims in this world, of course; far, far too many individuals who lack options and/or who did not in any meaningful sense choose or help create the situation in which they find themselves. And there are individuals whose learning histories are so distorted or incomplete that in the face of alternative options, they continue to choose the self-destructive. All of this is true, and true perhaps for all of us to some degree. The point here, however, is that it is possible to learn not to make victims of ourselves, not to make choices that are self-destructive; possible to acquire a learning history that supports the pursuit of personal development (as defined in Part I).

So, with the Free Choice Ethic, there is a slight of mind required: Apply this ethic to yourself but give others a wide berth. Assume that you have choice, that you are self-directing, that you are free to choose as you will. With that assumption, you push past unwarranted excuses and put yourself in a position to explore and perhaps expand the limits of your creativity. At the same time, recognize that the capacity for choice and self-direction is acquired, the result of a learning history that others may have yet to experience.

With that said, it is important to add that conduct in accord with the ethics of human development is one means for acquiring the learning history just discussed and for delivering that history to others. In fact, in many respects that is the purpose of the ethics of human development:

to provide the experience that educates, matures, and enlightens, increasing in the process freedom from the constraints of past conditioning and, so, the capacity to choose in accord with principle and enlightened self-interest. [22]

> *"Sometimes you get in a rut. It just feels like the world is against you. You want to blame somebody or something. That's understandable. We've all been there. And maybe you're right: The world is against you. I'm not going to pre-judge. Still, in my own case, I've been a bit premature with that conclusion."*

> *"My mother used to say: "No one is making you do this (whatever this is), you're choosing to do it. Now, cut it out!" I never forgot that. You can go around like you're a puppet, someone else holding the strings. Sometimes other people or other forces hold the strings, but a lot of the times we just act like they do. My mother never wanted me to be a victim of my own making. She was big on that."*

—Participant comments
Ethics of Human Development Training Program

"It is by not doing what they already know they should do that companies get into trouble over quality."

—Philip B. Crosby
Quality Without Tears

"Anybody possessing analytical knowledge recognizes the fact that the world is full of actions performed by people exclusively to their detriment and without perceptible advantage, although their eyes were open."

—Theodor Reik
Psychoanalyst and Author

". . . right is right, and wrong is wrong, and a body ain't got no business doing wrong when he ain't ignorant and knows better. It might answer for YOU to dig Jim out with a pick, WITHOUT any letting on, because you don't know no better; but it wouldn't for me, because I do know better."

Tom Sawyer to Huck Finn
—Mark Twain
The Adventures of Huckleberry Finn

The Conscious Mistakes Ethic

It is ethical to eliminate conscious mistakes. It is unethical to know that what you are about to do is wrong and to do it anyway.

Economist E. F. Schumacher wrote that work exists for the refinement of character.[23] This is one of the tenets to which the ethics of human development is anchored: the notion that work exists for the refinement of character and that working (*and living*) in accord with the ethics of human development refines character, evolves it, building the capacity for ever-larger motives to be expressed by and through the self.

One measure of this growth in capacity, this refinement of character, is the reduction of conscious mistakes. This refers not to a reduction in mistakes per se, but to the reduction in *conscious* mistakes.[24] Mistakes, in and of themselves, are one of the ways we learn. Through our mistakes, we gain clarity and become wise. Successful individuals often point to the number of mistakes they made until, at last, the successful route was discovered, the invention was made sound, the idea perfected. But no one becomes successful, wise, or more fully integrated by engaging in conscious mistakes. Rather, they and those around them are destroyed, at least by degree.

Perhaps we have misgivings about a given course of action. We think there are problems with it, but overall, we believe it to be the course of action we should take. If it turns out to be a mistake rather than the solution or result we had sought, then we will learn from our effort and choose differently next time. With conscious mistakes, however, we already know that the course of action upon which we are about to embark is a mistake, and still, we proceed.

Chuck Berry, the father of rock and roll, said, "Don't let the same dog bite you twice."[25] In so saying, he captured the spirit and reasoning embedded in the Conscious Mistakes Ethic. Many of us, figuratively speaking, can see ourselves in his statement: "Many times that dog has bitten me. Indeed, every time I have put my leg inside the fence—even though I have varied my approach, my voice, my dress—every time, he has bitten me. I know it is a mistake to put my leg inside the fence and yet, here I go again!"

While it is self-destructive to engage in conscious mistakes, it is extremely common to do so. They occur around the dessert tray all the time! They occur around the issue of diet, around exercise, relationships, the management of time and money. We know it is a mistake to consume this food, this next drink. And still, we eat it or drink it. Your body may be screaming for exercise. Or perhaps the screaming has died out, and still, you know that you need exercise. Yet you do nothing. This relationship or this job is a mistake and yet you do nothing to change it, modify it, alter it. You continue with it even though there is no doubt in your mind that as configured, this relationship or job is a mistake! In the world of work, potential examples abound: "I know it is a mistake not to contact this applicant's references... a mistake not to log my contacts with a given client... a mistake not to talk to my employee this very day about his performance. But still, I do not proceed."

None of these examples always fall into the category of conscious mistakes. One person's conscious mistakes are not necessarily another person's. Not until we proceed with what we know to be a mistake does our conduct fall into this category.

It is the rare person who eliminates conscious mistakes, just as it is a rare person who lives the totally ethical life. The point of the Conscious Mistakes Ethic is to reduce the frequency and variety of conscious mistakes in the direction of zero, confronting in the process the issues that continue to propel us toward self-destructiveness. *In fact, nothing so deepens the analysis of how we were made, programmed, conditioned as does the effort to figure out why we continue to do what we know we should not do.*[26]

Such an analysis takes us back through the stages of our development to the processes and events that shaped us, our sense of self, our trust, openness, confidence, our degree of self-regard, back to the issues that must be addressed if self-love is to prevail. Or perhaps we choose not to go back, but instead to move forward, starting now, with an attempt to build a new history through conduct anchored to principle rather than past conditioning. Conduct that redeems the past because it announces that even in that past, the seeds were present of the breakthrough now in evidence as old, self-destructive patterns are discerned and eliminated. Either way, we are served, consciousness expands, conscious mistakes are reduced.

One of the problems associated with not addressing and attempting to reduce conscious mistakes is that, through them, we flirt with the hardening of self-destructive habits—habits that, in the extreme, can lead to addiction. If addiction does occur, the problem becomes more complex, so complex that we are often hard put to untangle it alone. Hard put also to consider the addicted individual unethical simply because he continues to do what he knows he should not do. While conscious mistakes are unethical, addiction (which may or may not be the result of one's continuous indulging in conscious mistakes) is more like a train out of control, a mountain that may or may not be of one's own making, but which is enormously difficult to climb. To attempt to climb it—one step at a time, one day at a time, losing ground on some days but returning to climb again—is ethical and self-respecting. Indeed, to seek treatment in such circumstances is ethical. With addiction, a confluence of biological, psychological, spiritual factors operates, all related, perhaps, to an emptiness that must be filled, a craving for wellbeing that got distorted along the way and can now be repaired only gradually, step by step, as the overriding pangs of withdrawal give way to a renewed capacity for self-control. The person who, delirious from thirst, drinks saltwater is not unethical but confused by cravings a good deal more powerful than reason.[27]

Not only are conscious mistakes self-destructive, they are organizationally destructive, as well. As we are weakened, so too is every network of which we are a part. On the other hand, as we grow stronger and become increasingly whole, we bring strength and capacity to every network of which we are a part. If we were once our organization's weakest link, then its weakest link is no longer as weak and so, overall, the organization enjoys a new degree of wherewithal. Its center of gravity rises (as will be discussed in Part IV).

Reducing conscious mistakes requires and builds character—the point thus far—but it also accelerates the rate at which the validity of one's worldview is tested. Reducing conscious mistakes leads to a more complete testing of one's "map". It puts us in touch with the experience that results when conduct complies with current awareness and current beliefs. This allows us to assess, sooner rather than later, the legitimacy and worth of our view.

Say, for example, that you believe you should change your diet. Eat certain foods and not others. Your research has convinced you that there are benefits to be had. So, to not stick to the new diet, compromising it so often that you never test it, is to never know the value of that diet and those foods. In this area of your life, then, there is a discrepancy between what you say you should do and what you in fact do. The "should" is never tested or given a chance to evolve. It remains, and you remain caught in a compromise, a holding pattern created by your unwillingness to align conduct with current beliefs. Only by reducing conscious mistakes do we contact the errors in our map, aligning conduct with what experience announces is closer to the truth.[28]

Finally, to the extent that one adopts the ethics of human development, to not behave in accord with their requirements could be considered a conscious mistake. All ethics, then, reduced to this ethic that by itself steers conduct and refines character. "Perfection," wrote the writer Ken Carey, "is not the absence of mistakes but rather the absence of conscious mistakes."[29]

> "This is what ordinary people mean when they say that, although men (and women) may differ as to what things are right or wrong, no one ever thinks that it is right to do wrong or wrong to do right."
>
> —Wilbur Marshall Urban
> *Fundamentals of Ethics*

> *"Addiction, serious addiction is no joke. We had it in our family. It was hard on my brother. We almost lost him. But it was hard on everyone. We didn't know how to deal with it. We didn't even know what was going on at first."*
>
> *"If you want to go to the heart of the issue, I think you have to talk about how hard it is to stay conscious. We might know that it's a mistake to do this or that. We might say we aren't going to do it. But when the time comes, we go unconscious and do it anyway. Something takes over—our history, our habits, the pressure of the moment—and like a robot, we do what we have done in the past."*
>
> —Participant comments
> Ethics of Human Development Training Program

"One of the principles which determines our choice of one value over another, is that the permanent should be chosen over the transitory. Conservation, permanence, is a demand growing out of the very nature of value. Again, we say that it is difficult to give any meaning to the life of moral choice and effort, whether in the individual or the race, except on the assumption that there is progress or development towards perfection."

—Wilbur Marshall Urban
Fundamentals of Ethics

"What I do here matters. Everybody lives downstream."

—Robin Wall Kimmerer
Braiding Sweetgrass

The Sustainability Ethic

It is ethical to consider the long-range implications of your decision-making and to make sustainability a guiding tenet. It is unethical to knowingly implement practices that ensure the collapse or diminished health of self, organization, or environment.

The Sustainability Ethic encourages an awareness that what is done now will have implications for the future—indeed, will build the future for better or worse. So, with this ethic, sustainability is encouraged. Preserve and sustain planet Earth and its many interlocking regenerative processes so that this sphere, this spaceship, can continue to support life's flourishing. That is perhaps this ethic's first requirement.

But also preserve and sustain the cultural and personal practices that support self-realization, that allow an individual to continue to grow as a person, and that keep alive his ability to contribute to others safely, constructively, creatively over the long run. That, too, is a part of the Sustainability Ethic.

As philosopher Wilbur Marshall Urban wrote, "If the moral life were simply gathering water in a sieve, or rolling a stone up a hill, merely to have it roll back again, it would be essentially futile."[30] The presumption embedded in the Sustainability Ethic and in the ethics of human development overall is that the moral/ethical life is not futile but, rather, that it serves a larger end; namely, the full realization of life's inherent possibilities. Perhaps as one writer put it: "The purpose that throughout all history runs."[31]

The work of systems theorist John Platt on the nature of "traps" and "fences" can be helpful in clarifying the requirements of the Sustainability Ethic.[32] According to Platt, a trap is a situation in which short-term advantage is chosen at the cost of long-term disadvantage, short-term pleasure traded or embraced at the cost of long-term pain.

A *personal trap,* said Platt, is a situation in which the individual engages in behavior that has immediate or short-term advantages but long-term disadvantages. Examples might include smoking, overeating, eating unhealthy foods, excessive shopping, excessive drinking, criminal activity, perhaps even rudeness or punitive interpersonal tactics—any activity in which the rush, convenience, or pleasure comes with the future cost of discomfort, inconvenience, or pain.

An *organizational or social trap* is a situation in which the individual engages in behavior that has short-term advantages for the individual engaging in the behavior but immediate or long-term disadvantages for organization or society. The classic example here is what biologist Garrett Hardin called "the tragedy of the commons."[33]

A given farmer finds it to his advantage to graze an additional animal on the common pastureland. Eleven animals, though not ideal for market (but nearly so), bring a greater return than do ten animals fully ready for market. And so, an eleventh is added. This same logic, however, is followed by each farmer. Each adds an eleventh, a twelfth, a twentieth animal to the commons until it's carrying capacity collapses; that is, the pastureland is unable to regenerate its grasses given such heavy use and can no longer sustain any grazing at all. At that point, Platt would say, the trap closes and all the farmers, whether they contributed to the collapse or not, suffer the loss.

In today's world (and this was Hardin's point), the water, the air, the land, the Earth's regenerative processes are the commons. And when they are contaminated—their carrying capacity diminished—all suffer. This is the tragedy of the commons. And, as both Hardin and Platt point out, the collapse or contamination occurs as each individual or organization pursues short-term gains (pursued because there are short-term gains to be had) only to discover that, at some point, the larger system on which they depend is no longer capable of supporting them. The short-term interests of the individual or organization collide with the current or long-term interests of the collective, to the point that all, including those who initially profited, find themselves the victim of the collapse.

That is Platt's social trap: the way in which an individual's immediate or short-term interest, if pursued by enough individuals, can result in immediate or eventual trouble for all. Examples might include the polluting practices of some industries, the discharge of waste into public waterways, the excessive use of pesticides and fertilizers, the over-harvesting of the fishing and whaling industries, over-consumption in general, perhaps the sole allegiance of corporations to shareholders (as opposed to the recognition that employees, communities, and the environment are shareholders of a sort as well). And then there is climate change, the poisoning of the oceans, desertification. All of these constitute social and/or organizational traps in which narrow, short-term, individual focus, interest, or advantage lead to immediate or long-term collective disadvantage. Platt quotes Alexander Hamilton, who pointed out the nature of the problem in the *Federalist Papers*: "Momentary passions and immediate interests have a more active and imperious control over human conduct than general or remote considerations of policy, utility or justice."[34]

The opposite of a trap, in Platt's analysis, is a social or behavioral "fence." In these situations, short-term inconvenience or loss is traded or embraced for the sake of long-term convenience or gain. Examples of *personal fences* might include daily exercise, daily adherence to a healthy diet, meditation, deep relaxation, budgeting, comparative shopping, monotonous rehearsal of a skill or technique—any activity in which the individual must overcome her disinclination to engage in the activity enroute to enjoying its longer-term benefits.

An *organizational or social fence* is a situation in which behavior has immediate or short-term disadvantages for the individual but immediate or long-term advantages for organization or society. Examples might include conservation practices, the removing of an obstacle that has stopped traffic (with the hope that someone will let you back in once traffic begins flowing again), whistle-blowing, toll roads and bridges—activities or behaviors that may be inconvenient, costly, or even dangerous for the individual who engages in them, but that have immediate or long-term benefits for the organization or larger community.

> (NOTE: It should be noted that a fence may cease to be a fence for any number
> of reasons. Exercise or meditation, for example, may cease to be a fence once we
> find pleasure in the activity itself, not simply afterward or in the future; or, if not
> pleasure, then an understanding of the value of the activity so complete that we can

eliminate our resistance, leaving nothing between us and the practice of the activity
to overcome. In other words, what starts out as a fence can cease to be a fence as
the pleasure or understanding of the importance of the activity begins to align with
the knowledge of its future benefits.)

With Platt's concepts in mind, a restatement of the Sustainability Ethic is possible: *It is
ethical to submit all personal, organizational, cultural, and environmental practices to
scrutiny, altering them until they are as sustainable and free of traps as possible. It is
unethical to knowingly implement practices that ensure environmental collapse, and
unethical, as well, to implement practices that diminish the health and wellbeing of
individuals.*

So stated, it may be helpful to look more closely at the nature of the problem being addressed by the
Sustainability Ethic. It is the problem of self-control, implied with the other ethics but brought into
focus here. It is the problem of choosing between two rewards, one being offered now (that, if chosen,
will lead in the long run to suffering, i.e., a trap) and one that will come in the future (that requires
sacrifice now, i.e., a fence).

    If you are overweight and presented with the choice of eating sweets now or being thin now,
you will likely have little trouble choosing.[35] If you wish to be thin, you will choose the latter and that
will be that. The problem occurs when you have the choice between eating sweets now and achieving
your desired weight next year. With this choice, the temptation and challenge are great. It is the
commons example, or nearly so, from another angle.

    If we are given a choice between, on the one hand, doubling our income this year by using
pesticides that produce a toxic buildup in water and soil and, on the other hand, cultivation practices
that are sustainable but have only a modest impact on income, we will be tempted—especially if
everyone else in the region is choosing the former. Or say we are presented with the choice of
increasing profits by discharging effluents into the atmosphere or, alternatively, expending the amount
required to purify emissions. Which would we choose even though we know the latter supports a
clean environment and the former does not? What about the choice right now between exercise and
television, even though we are out of shape and value a healthy body? What about the choice between
the practice of our art and television or social media, even though we value our art and have not
practiced it for days or weeks? These are choice points, situations that pit the immediate against the
longer term. They are tests of self-control, as are ethics in general.

When an individual, organization, or industry is unable to regulate itself to the benefit of society,
society may attempt to redesign the incentive/disincentive arrangements under which the individual,
organization, or industry operates. To draw again from the work of Garrett Hardin: "Pipe the effluent
from the polluting smokestack into the ventilation system of the Board of Director's homes and
suddenly, decision-making reflects a broader, more 'environmentally friendly' concern. Put the
sewage outflow pipe upstream of the city's water intake pipe so that the city itself must contend with
its waste rather than leaving it for those downstream."[36] These examples illustrate the purpose of tax
incentive/disincentive programs, the establishment of superordinate regulatory authorities,[37] and full-

cost or true-cost accounting systems[38] in which the social and environmental costs are added to the other costs associated with production in order to determine the price of goods. All are attempts to align the short term with the long term so that individuals and organizations pay as they go, deferring nothing in the way of cost or cleanup for others. It is government or organizational arrangements[39] with the long run in mind, interventions designed to align current decision-making with sustainable ends. And it is necessary. Individual development is such that, without arrangements of this sort, the likelihood of conduct on behalf of others—ideally all others—and on behalf of an ecologically sane and sustainable future is highly unlikely.[40]

Finally, for those individuals who embrace the requirements of the Sustainability Ethic regardless of the presence or absence of external incentives, regardless also of the inconvenience or disadvantage it brings their way, there is unique status. Their sphere of concern has become life itself and their conduct a source of inspiration for those who recognize the strength and focus such conduct requires. We cannot realize the ethical life or, ultimately, our inherent possibilities without the capacity called for by this ethic, without the discipline to align present conduct with a future that is life supporting.

> *"As for keeping the long run in mind… you can appreciate how difficult it is for a society to do when you consider how hard it is for you to do. Exercise… eating the right foods… getting up early everyday so I can write or paint or study… all that's in my plan but sometimes, often times, I can't bring myself to do it."*

> *"I think it's particularly difficult when you're talking about forgoing personal conveniences or satisfactions for the sake of some longer-term group benefit. My family comes first. After that, it gets harder. Why am I forgoing what I want in my life for the sake of people I don't know, will never know, or for a future I will never see?"*

> *"I know this ethic is about the environment, about the responsible use of resources. There's so much involved in that topic… so much coordination of effort, putting in place the incentive structures that support the effort. That's something we haven't talked about enough, incentive structures. And yet, that, it seems to me, is at the heart of this discussion."*

> —Participant comments
> Ethics of Human Development Training Program

"No matter what anyone tells you, when you
lose business, it's almost always a relationship
problem."

> —James A. Autry
> *Love and Profit*

"However valid our assessment of our enemy's
destructiveness may be, we merely decrease our
creativity by fearing and hating them."

> —John David Garcia
> *Creative Transformation*

"Treat them all in a lofty manner lest they have
cause to find thee weak."

> —John Dee
> Eighteenth-Century Metaphysician
> Quoted in *Cosmic Trigger*
> by Robert Anton Wilson

The Wind Harp Ethic

It is ethical to treat others as you would like to be treated even though you are not always so treated. It is unethical not to find appropriate avenues for the expression of your anger, resentment, and rage to keep from passing them on to, or taking them out on, others. It is unethical to engage in scapegoating.

According to the Romantic poets, there existed in the Middle Ages an instrument called the wind harp.[41] Affix the wind harp to the window of your Middle Ages mud hut and wind entering the instrument from one side exited the other side as music. "We are wind harps!" exclaimed the Romantic poets. The idea being that it might be possible to so work on ourselves, so refine ourselves that no matter what "ill wind" blows our way, the anger, resentment, and/or rage produced in us is not passed on to others. The wind harp a metaphor for ending the cycle of violence.

Beyond that, however, the violence/violation not only not passed on to others but fully transformed; the anger, resentment, and rage turned into acts of beauty, acts so kind or full of grace that they can only be described as soulful. This is the full promise of the wind harp, a concept not unlike alchemy, the human being, sufficiently developed, an instrument for turning the life negating into the life enriching.

The Wind Harp Ethic requires that we not take out our negative emotions on others, either in the moment-to-moment sense in which we pass on the abuses of everyday life to others or in the generational sense in which the violence done to one generation is passed on to the next.

Alice Miller, student of child-rearing practices worldwide, argued that to move the world in the direction of peace, stop battling your parents on the battleground of your own children.[43] If you had violence and abuse visited upon you as a child, though your anger is justified, liberate your children by not visiting that same violence on them.

In well-known experiments from the 1960s, one of two monkeys placed in the same cage is shocked repeatedly (a mild electric shock). Soon, the monkey that is shocked begins hitting, scratching, and otherwise abusing the other innocent by-standing monkey. This is primate behavior, primate logic. It is perhaps the paradigm of the bully, the spouse-beater, the individual who comes home and kicks the dog. It is one way to account for the rage and violence spewed in the direction of the nearest, least likely to retaliate victim—not infrequently, a loved one.

In organizations, we see the absence of the Wind Harp Ethic in the passing on of a negative mood or attitude to others. The supervisor treats her employee rudely. That employee, in turn, treats her own employees rudely. They then treat fellow workers rudely, and the climate of the organization becomes negative overnight. Those who insist that leadership sets the tone and is therefore solely responsible for organizational morale are giving away too much. Leadership plays its role, but the Wind Harp Ethic argues implicitly that our morale is far too precious a commodity for it to be made dependent on others, even organizational leaders.

Linked with the notion of the wind harp is Gandhi's admonition to "Be the change you expect,"[43] i.e., the change you would like to see in others, especially if you expect or would like to see courtesy, respect, and ongoing personal development.

Of course, to succeed with Gandhi's admonition, or to successfully incorporate the capacity of the wind harp, means that we must control our reaction to our feelings. Experience our feelings, acknowledge their legitimacy, but control our reaction to them. John David Garcia defines neurosis as "having feelings or emotions that interfere with your ability to accomplish your purpose."[44] The Wind Harp Ethic requires the mastering of our reaction to our feelings so that purpose, vision, the ideal can more often hold sway regardless of what ill wind is blowing.

Any number of activities can prove helpful in our effort to control our reaction to our feelings. Exercise, meditation, gardening, the many art forms available to humans, the study of great and enduring ideas, service to others, spiritual practices of one sort or another, time spent in nature, individual and group therapies, creativity in general—all can be helpful. Each can provide a safe and constructive way to restore balance to our perspective, perhaps building a sturdiness that makes it less likely that we will lose track of our purpose as powerful emotions come and go.

Finally, to reiterate: to succeed even by degree with the embracing of the Wind Harp Ethic is to benefit both ourselves and others. We spare others the indiscriminate spewing or inappropriate targeting of anger and rage, and we become less neurotic, less likely to give ourselves reason for recrimination and self-loathing because we made innocent people pay for our frustration. We give ourselves hope, esteem, optimism, as even slight success at controlling our reaction to our feelings begins to undercut the notion that we cannot be responsible for how we behave. Anger, resentment, humiliation, rage do occur, but to not take those feelings out on others who had nothing to do with them is empowering. More empowering still is to not take those feelings out on those who *did* have something to do with them, and instead to act from reason, with forethought, compassion, the long run in mind.

There is great artfulness in this, the mastery of the self. Child-rearing requires it; as does teaching. And leadership. With this ethic, the meaning of personal responsibility is expanded to include composure, equanimity, an increasing ability to not take events personally. Both detachment and interior peace are needed so that choice remains in play, so we can choose wisely our response rather than react robotically, though understandably, to life's affronts.

> *"I was telling an old friend what we're doing, and he asked me point blank if I really thought people can change. He said he has known people for thirty years, forty years, and they're the same today as when he met them. Wiser? Meaner? More generous? He didn't think so. I argued with him, and he finally acknowledged that people do change sometimes, but he wasn't optimistic. He's a cynical fellow. I encouraged him to address one of his own limitations. Change himself in some desirable way, and see if his experience changes his optimism about others. I haven't heard back."*

—Participant comment
Ethics of Human Development Training Program

"The measure of individuals—and so of corporations— is the extent to which we struggle to complete ourselves, the energy we devote to living up to our potential."

—Max DePree
Leadership Is an Art

"No organization can be more progressive or more effective than its people."

—Henry Ford II
The Human Environment and Business

"Withdraw into yourself and look. And if you do not find yourself beautiful yet, act as does the creator of a statue that is to be made beautiful; he cuts away here, he smoothes there, he makes the line lighter, this other purer, until a lovely face has grown upon his work. So do you also: . . . never cease chiseling your statue."

—Plotinus (AD 205?–270)
Quoted in *A Guide for the Perplexed*
by E. F. Schumacher

The Personal Growth Ethic

It is ethical to continue to grow as a person, to continue to increase your capacity to conduct yourself in accord with your ethics and principles. It is unethical to stop growing as a person, to not continue the lifelong process of personal/ psychological/spiritual growth.

The Personal Growth Ethic calls on us to take responsibility for our continuing growth as persons. It's admonition: grow, learn, expand awareness, refine character. Find the higher reaches of human development that give joy and perspective in the face of hardship. To do so is self-honoring, and honoring as well of those we love, as it puts before them an example that makes their conclusion that they cannot do the same less and less tenable.

Each of us is part of a community, and within that community a part of many organizations, from family to workplace to volunteer center. To continue to grow as a person is to render ourselves increasingly valuable to the organizations of which we are a part. As we mature, we are better able to serve them, better able to help them accomplish their purpose.

Further, to continue to grow as a person is to put before our families, friends, and coworkers an example of what we would ask of them. Our credibility increases (since we can do what we would have them do), and so, too, our optimism and the optimism of those we care about. For if we can continue to grow psychologically and spiritually, though inertia and the forces of entropy insist we stop, then both we and our friends, who know us so well, may conclude that they can do so as well. Thus, in this not so obvious way, conduct in accord with this ethic is of service to others as well as to ourselves.

Of course, to grow as a person takes time. And while this may be obvious, we often behave—toward ourselves if not toward others—as if change should occur overnight. We fail to acknowledge that the changes we are attempting to bring about in ourselves can be extremely difficult given that we may be contending with long-entrenched habits of thinking and doing, incentives and disincentives locking in place the current holding pattern. Difficult also given the scarring that can come from childhood abuse and/or dysfunctional upbringings in general.

To bring about desired and desirable change given these factors requires time, not to mention a certain compassionate and bemused regard for our resistance even to the change we believe good for us. Therefore, it is not weakness or a lack of belief in who and what we are to admit that we sometimes need help and should not be shy about seeking it. Therapy, in many of its forms, can be helpful, as can workshops and seminars devoted to interior development, the expansion of awareness, the cultivation of mindfulness, the practice of meditation. Higher education of the sort that is available through great books, great teachers, the arts, the study of philosophy, the study of excellence or quality in general, the daily practice of a spiritual discipline designed to quiet the mind and/or cultivate a reverence for life—all of these can be extremely helpful. The only proviso with any of these is that they must be attempted in earnest, as even these activities can function as escapes from the difficult issues that must be addressed if growth is to be served. When attempted in earnest, however, and with the open-mindedness of Ethic 2, these forms of self-help can be pivotal, giving us at the very least perspective and perhaps the strength to maintain that perspective—one infused with kindness and a loving regard for our own halting efforts to grow as persons.

Lastly, it is by means of this ethic that we align ourselves with the biological imperative that grew us from infancy to adulthood and now, through our conscious intervening, continues our development forward to the higher levels discussed in Part I. The autonomous self decides whether development is to continue. And as development continues, marked by the increasing capacity for ethical conduct and self-direction, there comes as well, perhaps, a reduced sense of alienation, of what Owen Barfield called *cutoffness.* Continued development leads eventually to the Mature-Minded individual discussed in Part I for whom the separation between self and other—functionally speaking—dissolves. At that level, the individual treats others as he would treat himself because the self with whom he identifies has enlarged to include them. And he treats them well, which is to say with regard for their own highest attainment, because he so likes and respects the self. This may be the height of ethical development, a state of being that makes the unethical increasingly untenable because what we are doing to others is what we are doing to ourselves.

> *"Yes, the Personal Growth Ethic . . . The "know thyself" thing. Becoming kinder, more compassionate, quicker to laugh, braver… Also, less constrained or sad or held back. It just seems like the whole personal growth thing comes down to that, and then allowing what happens—all the many things that result from what you do—to enlighten you further."*

> *"Organizations, families, communities… their primary focus, at least their self-serving focus, as far as I am concerned, should be on the ethical and creative growth of the individuals that comprise them. What else? All the problems society faces, the world faces, whatever else is done to address those problems, it's all for naught unless we also become, each of us, more of what we are capable of being. That's the point here, right?"*

—Participant comments
Ethics of Human Development Training Program

"There is only one real deprivation, I decided this morning, and that is not to be able to give one's gift . . . The gift turned inward, unable to be given, becomes a heavy burden, even sometimes a kind of poison. It is as though the flow of life were backed up."

—May Sarton
Poet and Novelist
Quoted in *The Gift*
by Lewis Hyde

"The gift is to the giver, and comes back most to him [or her]—it cannot fail . . ."

—Walt Whitman
19th Century American Poet
From "Carol of Words"

"When man gives, 'the stream of life continues to flow'. . .'"

—Gerardus Van der Leeuw
Historian and Philosopher
Quoted in *Escape From Evil*
by Ernest Becker

The Gift-Sharing Ethic

It is ethical to utilize your gifts, talents, and unique experience on behalf of others. Through the expression of your unique gifts, you may help others evolve and, in the process, acquire for yourself a greater sense of purpose and meaning. It is unethical not to share your gifts, talents, and unique experience somewhere, for the benefit of someone.

The final operating assumption of the ethics of human development is that each of us, either by virtue of birth (though that is rare) or through the living of life, acquires some insight, talent, unique bit of experience or knowledge that can be of benefit to others, that may aid them in their development. We acquire a "gift." And the giving of this gift to at least one other person for their benefit is the requirement of the Gift-Sharing Ethic.[45]

Some people have acquired grand gifts, gifts and talents that require a stage, a platform from which the display of their gift brings joy, pleasure, and insight to many. Others have acquired gifts that play better one-on-one, person-to-person, parent and grandparent to child, friend to friend. But whatever the nature of our gift, it is vital that we share it with at least one other person for their benefit. Philosopher/inventor Buckminster Fuller said that you can assume that you are fulfilling your purpose if you are in the process of turning your experience into products and events that bring advantage to others.[46] That is the essence of the Gift-Sharing Ethic, the reasoning—the human logic—behind it.

Through the sharing of our gift with at least one other person, we bring advantage to them. They benefit in whatever way is afforded by our gift (our knowledge, our insight, our creation). But as Fuller indicates, we benefit as well. We gain a measure of fulfillment, a sense that our life, whatever the twists and turns and however wrongheaded it may have seemed at times, is nevertheless amounting to something—because here is another person benefiting from what we have distilled and are able to convey.

When consciously engaged, the parent, the teacher, the mentor is, by definition, fulfilling the requirements of this ethic. And perhaps it could be argued that this is one aspect of our evolutionary assignment: to parent, teach, and mentor one another to greater wholeness or maturity and, in the process, gain a measure of the same for ourselves.

In our organizations, our workplaces, there is the ongoing opportunity to accommodate the requirements of this ethic.

The following addition to one's job description, whatever the job, puts the spirit of this ethic front and center:

And lastly, the individual holding this position should re- create it. He/she should make it new. The new version should include all that the organization found useful in the previous version while adding for the first time what is now possible given

This addition to the standard job description calls on us to engage in our work fully, drawing on and utilizing our unique gifts, whatever they are, to evolve the workplace and in the process, create for ourselves a greater degree of job/life satisfaction. At base, it announces that we are to work consciously. And that means, among other things, with an eye out for what our history and unique talents permit us to contribute.

Of course, there may be no room or interest in our organization or workplace for what we believe we can contribute beyond, simply, the doing of the job, the nature of the work or our position such that we find it impossible to add what is unique to us. But even if this is so, still we must find someone somewhere who is interested in what we have to offer and serve that person and ourselves by extending our gift. That is the requirement of this ethic.

In his book *The Gift*, Lewis Hyde wrote that gift-giving of the sort we are discussing recognizes, establishes, and maintains community.[47] The health of a community, he argues, is gauged by the amount of gift-giving occurring within it. Gift-giving a measure of the vitality residing in the community, a measure of its interest in and capacity for further development, synergic development—as synergy is possible only with the flow and exchange of ideas, knowledge, and resources.

The death of a group, on the other hand, is marked by the absence of the creative exchange of gifts, art, and/or knowledge.[48] Thus, gift-giving is life-giving.[51] When gift-giving occurs, individuals feel honored, present in the awareness of others, and so less defensive, less alienated, more able to contribute their own gifts. When we consciously attempt to share what is most essential to us—our truest insight, talent, or art, with sensitivity and respect, recognizing that those with whom we are sharing are deeply deserving—we fight the emptiness and even the despair that can seep into the lives of those we care about, and into our own lives, as well.

Finally, one last point concerning this ethic, which may extend to the ethics of human development overall: What is the most fundamental gift we have been given, the gift necessary, though not sufficient, for all other gifts? It would not be surprising if we were to conclude that *time* is that gift. That conclusion, coupled with the fact that this gift is of unknown and limited duration, can have a quickening effect on consciousness. For some, it is the heightened sense of time that marks the beginning of the ethical life. With no time to waste, how are we to use the time that remains? The answer, implicit throughout the discussion of the ethics of human development, is intentionally, meaningfully, to the benefit of others, allowing us to conclude that our time is well spent.

The fulfillment of purpose: that is what concerns us when the sense of mortality cuts to the core. The full life requires purpose, the giving of one's gift, the turning of one's experience to the benefit of others. And the human logic embedded in this line of thought, and in the Gift-Sharing Ethic itself, announces that we are benefited in return.

"Man is built to be an individual incarnation of the whole," wrote Jacob Needleman in his introduction to the *Tao Te Ching*. "His good, his happiness—the very meaning of his life—is to live in correspondence and relationship to the whole. . .."[50] The ethics of human development are an attempt to help us acquire—however gradually—that kind of relationship to the whole. And the Gift-Sharing Ethic is the ethic that calls on us to give back by contributing to others, and thus, to the whole that gives each part meaning.

> *"Traditional Onondaga understand a world in which all*
> *beings were given a gift, a gift that simultaneously*
> *engenders a responsibility to the world."*
>
> —Robin Wall Kimmerer
> *Braiding Sweetgrass*

> *"Well, I'll be honest with you. I thought the ethics were sort of obvious. I mean, maybe I heard them taught in other words but, frankly, I knew this stuff a long time ago."*
>
> *"Yeah, maybe, but what does it mean to <u>know</u> something? My grandfather used to say: When it comes to some things, you don't know it unless you can do it... unless you can live it. You can say you know this stuff, and maybe you do. But my grandfather would say that a lot of us, even at his age, don't know it yet."*
>
> —Participant comments
> Ethics of Human Development Training Program

SUMMARY

In the last book before his death, Buckminster Fuller wrote: "Humanity is now maintaining an unstable collection of local holding patterns, awaiting a physical or metaphysical integrity to give structure to the future and to show the way out of the darkness."[51] If by structure is meant a set of rules for guiding behavior in a direction we value, the ethics of human development offer one such structure. And we do value our own development. We value the transcending of limits, personal or otherwise, because we value the greater freedom that results. New limits also result, but in time, we value their transcending as well. The direction is toward greater freedom or wholeness, toward a growing repertoire that allows us to be at ease with ourselves (and also ethically creative) in an ever-expanding circle of people, situations, and settings.

That is the final point made in this section. The ethics of human development are a means for enlarging the field of play and, along with it, our capacity to perform effectively on it. They are the rules for addressing directly the forces that establish limits (i.e., ignorance and fear), the rules for gathering the experience that leads to the transcending of those limits. Everyone is interested in a way out of the darkness, in finding the illumination that makes for greater ease of navigation, greater understanding, so that the desired difference or contribution can be made. The ethics of human development are one way of addressing that interest. They are a means for assuming responsibility for our own development and for assisting constructively in the development of others.

We are all issued a call to being. This call is answered with birth, but neither the call nor the need for an answer ends there. "To be or not to be" remains the question throughout our lives. The ethics detailed here are one way of continuing to answer that call in the affirmative, a way of announcing our interest in and commitment to being, and to being more in the everyday world where it matters so much. This is ethics as human logic, ethics by which we educate, mature and enlighten ourselves. To behave in accord with these ethics is to make more likely a future where human development and flourishing, and not something less than that, is the principal value.

Part III

Dilemmas from Work & Everyday Life

"All the world's a stage . . ."

—William Shakespeare, *As You Like It*

Schumacher's question: *Where is The Good situated and how it is reached?* Part I argues that The Good is found in the realization of our full potential as human beings. Part II argues that The Good is reached and expressed through conduct in accord with the ethics of human development. Part III expands the answer provided in Part II.

The assumption underlying Part III is this: We are made via our interaction with the environment. Most specifically, through how we choose to address the dilemmas that come our way.

The ethics of human development provide guidance. They impose a standard. Proceed in accord with that standard, we are saying, and you gather the experience most likely to educate and mature you, the experience that will tell you who you are *now...* and perhaps, what you must do to reach and more often embody your full developmental potential.

That is the more exact answer to the second part of Schumacher's question. To restate: Development toward The Good depends on how we choose to address the tests of heart and mind that come our way, ethical dilemmas large and small, and by how we choose to respond to the results of our efforts. We are back to "life as morality play."

ALL THE WORLD'S A STAGE

The training program on which much of this book is based (The Ethics of Human Development Training Program—more about this in Part V) contains a number of role-playing scripts and theater-like exercises that bring to life common everyday dilemmas.

What follows is a selection of these role-playing scripts. Several are from the world of work and may appear small in magnitude. Still, they pose a dilemma for at least one person in the "scene". How that person responds is likely to affect not only that person's development, however slightly, but the development—certainly the experience—of others in the scene, and, by degree, the development of the surrounding culture whether of workplace, family, or community.

Before beginning, one last critical point: From the world of horse racing comes a useful analogy. Toward the end of every race, if the possibility of winning is sensed, the jockey "asks" his mount to go for the win. This asking can come in many forms. A movement of the reins, vocal cues, the showing of the whip; in whatever way it comes, jockeys refer to it as *the posing of the question.*[1]

For the sake of our own development, *we must learn to recognize when the question is being posed.* Considering situations that offer even a slight developmental/ethical challenge—as is the case with several of the "scenes" that follow—can be helpful in that regard.

<u>Scene 1</u>: *The Play within the Play*

Two individuals are visiting in the hallway during a break in a staff training session.

Rex: That's what I hate about these staff training sessions.

Will: What do you mean?

Rex: I mean, tell me about my job, but spare me the rest. I'm here to do a job, not join a club. Organizational values! My values are just fine, thank you. I don't need to know about the "big picture" or whatever it is they're talking about in there!

Will: I don't know, Rex. I sort of like hearing about how this place is organized, what everybody else is doing, the stuff they think we should know.

Rex: Well, help yourself. You'll forget it in a week, and you'll see then that it doesn't make any difference.

Will: You know, see how the whole thing fits together.

Rex: Do your job and collect your pay. That's how it fits together.

Will: Well, what if—

Rex: It's a waste of time! We could be focusing on our own jobs, doing our own work right now. This is just stealing time. Maybe if you were the president of the company or something like that, but at our level, what does it matter?

Will: Well, it's time to go back in. The session is starting.

Rex: Time to work on my doodling!

Staff training, education, schooling of any sort presents a dilemma to those attending, especially if the relevance of what is being taught is in doubt. Participants can hear themselves say privately, if not to others: "Why should I have to do this? This is a waste of time!"

The scenes under consideration in Part III are presented without context. In this scene, for example, we do not know the history of staff training in this organization, or the history of the individuals involved. There could be some truth to what Rex is saying. He may have found little value in previous staff training sessions.

Still, staff training is an opportunity for all who attend because it puts choice and attitude front and center. It is the play within the play, an opportunity to exhibit and exercise the attitude we bring to work, and perhaps, at times, to life.

"I'll attend the session, but I'm going to do the absolute minimum... work on other things." Or perhaps: "I'm going to take issue with everything... the trainer, the material, the timing of the breaks, you name it. This is ridiculous and I'm not going to let them know it!"

To varying degrees, we all have been that person: arms folded, wearing a perpetual frown, looking for mistakes, whispering discontent to those around us. That person is in each of us—or can be—and we must get very good at detecting the moment that person shows up in us. Detect and self-correct, with compassion but with little patience, for this attitude serves only to harm us and the organization. It is a violation of several ethics of human development at once, if not all of them.

When Rex adopts his stance, he presents Will with a dilemma. Will, who seems to embrace the training event for what it might offer, is left with the choice of what to do. *The question is being posed.* He does offer Rex reasons for why the training might be of value. And he remains true to his own view, not going over to Rex's side when others might have done so. Beyond that, maybe he thinks the way Rex is behaving is not worth the bother—Rex just being Rex—and in the course of things, what does it matter? On the other hand, if the content of the training is important, or if how one approaches training is important (affecting, for example, the training experience for others), then what Rex is choosing to do is, to some degree, harming the organization.

Maybe Will feels he has done all that is reasonable and if more is needed, it's an issue for Rex's supervisor, not a colleague or teammate. Still, if Will cares about the organization and cares about Rex, he may wonder if he could do more, whether he might find a thoughtful, assertive, or humorous way of calling Rex to the approach that would make the team stronger—the playful or serious nudging that says: "Let's do this and get what we can from it." Of course, if Will decided to take that approach—a challenge given Rex's attitude—it would have to be done skillfully, born of a desire to create and be a part of an organization worthy of its members—with members who, in turn, insist that they and their colleagues are worthy of it.

> *"Why should Will say anything to Rex? It's not Will's job to adjust Rex's attitude... Rex's attitude is Rex's problem. And his boss's problem."*
>
> *"They're teammates, right? I've played sports all my life... teammates tell each other all the time to shape up. If you want a better team, you speak up."*
>
> —Participant comments
> Ethics of Human Development Training Program

(NOTE: The above scene may seem incidental as things go. Is too much being made of it? Not in the view presented here. Rather it is in the fine grain of everyday life, with situations so seemingly small, that a good deal of self-making occurs. Can you see what is going on? Can you recognize when the question is being posed? Do you have the willingness and skill to turn it in another direction? Thank goodness for the small matters. Through them—providing we are observant—we learn who we are; and through them, if we so choose, we build capacity for ethically addressing the larger matters sure to come along.)

<u>Scene 2</u>: *Making Work for Others*

Two individuals within an organization are finishing a job and are anxious to go home. This scene could occur in a school, a university, a corporation, a studio, a ranch, a construction site, etc.

Jake: Well, Mike, does that do it?

Mike: That does it. And about time, wouldn't you say?

Jake: Come on, let's get outta here.

Mike: I'm with you, just as soon as I put this equipment away and tidy up a bit.

Jake: Are you kidding? I've come in plenty of times and found this place in worse condition than this.

Mike: It'll only take a minute. Besides, I've seen the morning schedule. It's pretty tight.

Jake: Look, I wasn't hired to clean this place up. Let's go. They'll deal with it in the morning. We could be thirty minutes putting this stuff away.

Mike: Yeah, but they could be put out at us for leaving this.

Jake: They'll get over it. Chances are it will all be forgotten by the time we get in tomorrow. Nobody will say anything. You'll see. Now let's go!

Ethic 1, Corollary 4 states that it is unethical to make work unnecessarily harder for others. That may be what happens in this scenario if Mike has his way.

Jake, therefore, is confronted with a dilemma (presuming he embraces Ethic 1, Corollary 4). What he chooses to do will have implications for himself and very likely, for others in the organization. If he goes along with Mike, knowing that he is making work for others, , then his self-respect will be diminished, at least by degree. He will have given in to expedience or social pressure at the expense of what he believes is right.

As for the impact on others... Maybe, as Mike says, nothing will come of it, nothing will be said. But even if nothing is said, making work for others can breed resentments.

Is there nothing that Jake can do to turn the situation in the direction of what he thinks is right? Is he too tired, weak, or forgetful to act on his own behalf? Is Mike's approval more important to him than his allegiance to himself, his family, the organization on which he and his family depend? Or does he simply not see the moment for what it is until later, when someone complains?

Whatever the case, Jake has these questions to consider. Providing that he permits the self-examination these questions invite, he will be the better for it, perhaps resolving to do differently next time. And if he does do differently next time, he will have used his experience to the benefit of himself and others. On the other hand, if he avoids the self-review, avoids the resolution to do differently next time, avoids even raising a question concerning end-of-shift responsibilities, then it is hard to imagine that he is making anything but trouble for himself and others down the road. Whatever Jake chooses, however, it is worth emphasizing (as was done with the previous scene) that it is here, in situations so seemingly small, that the opportunity for self-making occurs. Here, also—in situations of no greater magnitude than what Jake and Mike are experiencing—where the culture of the organization is felt and, depending on the choices made, furthered along or gradually undone.

> *"Mike could have talked until he was blue in the face and Jake was not going to change his stance. I don't think there's anything Mike could have said that would have changed the situation."*
>
> *"This issue goes as deep as you want to take it. Efficiency. Flexibility. Common courtesy, the potential for resentment, even anger, they're all wrapped up in this corollary. Make work unnecessarily harder and all those concerns come into play."*
>
> —Participant comments
> Ethics of Human Development Training Program

<u>Scene 3</u>: *Personal Responsibility / Self-examination*

Two old friends on a walk. Steeped in conversation. Late afternoon.

Fred: *You're doing it to yourself.*

Leon: *Doing it to myself... Please!*

Fred: I'm your best friend. I've been your best friend since we were kids.

Leon: *Where are you going with this?*

Fred: No one else will tell you.

Leon: Why are you telling me?

Fred: Because I know we'll be friend's no matter what.

Leon: Doing *what* to myself?

Fred: You moan and complain about your failed relationships, about the difficulty of keeping employees, on and on.

Leon: I don't know what you're talking about. I haven't met the right person. That's the story there. And as for my business... do you have any idea how hard it is to find decent employees?

Fred: *Every relationship has been the ONE!* That is, until it wasn't. And your employees... There's a pattern.

Leon: And you see the pattern and I don't, is that it?

Fred: We're from the same neighborhood., Leon. I know what you've overcome. What we've all overcome. It hasn't been easy.

Leon: What's that got to do with anything?

Fred: It's not working, right? You tell me that every time we get together. And what I'm telling you is: *It's not them. It's you.*

Leon: *It's always them, my friend. It's never us. Or have you forgotten?*

Fred: That was then. When we were young. It seemed like it was always them. But times have changed. I've changed. You've changed. *It's not always "them" anymore.*

The Open-Mindedness Ethic: *The possibility that we may not be right. That our view is incomplete, including our view of ourselves.* The Feedback Ethic: *The giving, as needed, of negative or corrective feedback.*

What is our responsibility to our friends? To our loved ones? According to ethicist John David Garcia: "When we love someone, we must give them clear and unavoidable negative feedback when they are destructive, recognizing that they may be right and that we may be in error. If they refuse this feedback or its intent, then their own fear will drive them away from us."[2]

Fred cares about Leon. So much so that he is willing to run the risk of rejection, of being told to mind his own business. He is willing to say to Leon that he (Leon) is his own worst enemy.

It's possible that Fred is wrong about this but he is willing to risk it. Perhaps you could say, willing to address what he sees as his ethical obligation to his friend.

Can Leon be open to what Fred is saying, can he hear it? Can he respond constructively? That is the question being posed to Leon.

> *"Leon is lucky to have Fred as a friend. Fred didn't back down. He didn't let it go. He continued to try to reach his friend. That's friendship in my book."*

> *"It seems like the "openness" theme would have to include a willingness to engage in self-reflection. I happen to think that it is sometimes "them", pure and simple. But it is sometimes "us", as well. If you're closed off to that possibility, then you're partially blind."*

—Participant comments
Ethics of Human Development Training Program

Scene 4: *The Creative Culture*

Two coworkers come across one another in the hall, or in the lunchroom, or in the elevator, etc.

Jill:	Hey, Carl, I've been thinking about you. What's going on?
Carl:	Nothing much. Same old routine, really. What's going on with you?
Jill:	Everything's just great! Say, Carl, whatever happened to that idea of yours?
Carl:	What idea is that?
Jill:	You know, the one about scheduling.
Carl:	Forget it.
Jill:	Forget it? What do you mean? You were all fired up about it a week ago.
Carl:	Yeah, well, they really know how to put out the fire around here.
Jill:	You mean they shot it down?
Carl:	I mentioned it, figuring they'd go for it . . . All they wanted were facts and figures. Turned the whole thing into a huge obstacle.
Jill:	Well, that's not so surprising, is it? I mean it was a basic change you were proposing. Maybe they just wanted to make sure that everything was covered.
Carl:	Look, this place is afraid of anything and everything that is out of the usual. I think the idea scared them. I learned my lesson.
Jill:	Your lesson?
Carl:	I'm saving my ideas for after work. This place will never change.
Jill:	Yeah, I know what you mean. They say they want your ideas, but as soon as you come up with one—
Carl:	They get a big frown on their face.
Jill:	Anyway, where are you off to now, Carl?
Carl:	Well, believe it or not, I'm attending staff development's workshop on creativity.
Jill:	You're kidding!
Carl:	I'm not kidding. But don't worry. I'm one guy who knows the score.

In this scene, Jill is met with a dilemma. At first, she stands up for the possibility that the requests made by Carl's superiors when he presented his idea were reasonable and that they may be thinking of potential implications of which Carl is unaware. Perhaps they simply want to ensure the likely success of the proposed idea... elaboration needed before they can take it seriously. The mere fact that they have asked for elaboration a sign that the idea has promise.

It is true that we don't know what has happened to Carl (or perhaps to others that Carl knows) when ideas have been presented in the past. Maybe they have been good ideas, or maybe they haven't been good ideas—that, too, is possible. Maybe his ideas have been shot down or put aside. Or maybe they have simply fallen on deaf ears. Whatever the case, Carl apparently believes that he cannot contribute to the organization as he would like, that his creative ideas for improvement are not welcome.

This raises a pivotal dilemma for Carl. Is the organization worthy of the life he wants to give it? Does he have the time and energy apart from his other tasks to follow up on his ideas for change? And if not, can he remain a member of the organization without losing his commitment to it? If he must leave, can he do so without damage, without the burning of bridges, finding in the process an organization to which he can contribute as he would like?

In the beginning, Jill encourages Carl to extend the benefit of the doubt. But as Carl continues with his indictment, Jill joins in and, in so doing, gives support to Carl's disgruntlement. The Organizational Ethic, Corollary 8: *It is ethical to create organizational improvements, unethical not to help the organization evolve.* This is based on the notion that organizations grow, evolve, and remain relevant through creative work—that creative work gives life to the organization. But it is based also on the notion that individuals grow and evolve through their effort to work creatively, to formulate and implement creative change. This is what Jill's dilemma is about. Initially, she supports a culture of personal responsibility, of personal growth in which neither Carl nor his superiors are assumed to be incompetent or wrong, in which more creative work may be all that is needed on Carl's part. She then changes her position and falls in league with Carl, creating in the process a subculture in which cynicism and blaming prevail.

This change in Jill's position raises for her an issue worth considering. Why, she might ask herself, did she change her allegiance in the middle of this exchange? We do not know Jill's history with Carl or with the organization any more than we know Carl's. Nor do we know the history or character of the organization. But what good does Jill do Carl or the organization by supporting Carl in his withdrawal? She only avoids her own challenge, failing herself as she fails to say to Carl (in whatever way she finds best) that no one is keeping him from being creative; that even here he can continue to create, and, if not here, then elsewhere. And in any event, he should remember that what he is ultimately creating (whatever his work might be) is the upkeep of his own morale, which is certain to diminish if he does not behave in ways that nourish it.

Ultimately, the dilemma that confronts both Carl and Jill has to do with the victimization of the self. Instead of finding a way to create the change they desire; or accepting the fact that the desired change cannot be created now given their time, energy, and the organization as it stands; or creating a way to leave because that is the self-honoring thing to do, Carl and Jill complain. And by complaining, which leads not to action but only to more complaining, they make victims of themselves. At some level, they cannot help but be depressed about the option they have selected. Instead of exercising their power to create, they slip into anger—anger at themselves (though this might be unconscious) and at the organization. In the sharing of their disgruntlement, they form a small culture not of growth but of commiseration, a situation in which the feedback and support they provide one another keeps them oblivious to the harm they are doing to themselves and the organization.

The Personal Growth Ethic: *"It is ethical to continue to grow as a person, to engage in those activities that support and are likely to result in psychological/ethical development, unethical to stop growing as a person, to settle for less than we deserve and are capable of becoming."* This is the ethic in question for Carl and Jill, the ethic in question with all the dilemmas presented in Part III. How we choose to interact in these situations provides us with the information we use to assemble our self-understanding, our self-knowledge—the information we use to define ourselves. This is why ethical dilemmas even of the size we are describing are so important. Like the individuals in the previous scenes, Carl and Jill are engaging in self-defining behavior, driving home (albeit perhaps subliminally) their conclusion concerning the stuff of which they are made. By what they choose to do, they are building and reinforcing a self-concept—as are we all. Through interactions with ethical dilemmas, small and relatively minor though they may seem, the self is made (or the self-concept is made), and with it the sense of who and what one is and, also, the sense of what one might become given the influence and potential control individuals have over their own making.

> *"I think you're being a bit harsh. I mean, this was just a brief exchange between co-workers, a small matter. Jill was empathetic. Why should she have the burden of addressing the situation on behalf of the organization"?*

> *"It's on her behalf, as well, right? That's what we've been saying. Even in these scripts, small and incidental though they may seem, individuals are making themselves bit by bit. Forming, constructing their sense of identity while also building, in the process, the organization's culture."*

—Participant comments
Ethics of Human Development Training Program

<u>Scene 5</u>: *Feedback and the Observing Self*

Two people are discussing a meeting that has just ended. They are peers within a large organization.

Alicia: Well, frankly, I think I said exactly what I needed to say.

Harold: Well, it's just that—

Alicia: Look, if it's junk, it's junk. Why should I pamper him?

Harold: I know, but we need everyone—

Alicia: All I said was that his idea had been tried before and that we all had to do better than that. And that's the truth.

Harold: I was there. He hadn't finished before you were shuffling through papers, raising your eyebrows, cutting him off. You wouldn't like it if it had been the other way around.

Alicia: You know what he was proposing. We tried that same idea two years ago, and it didn't work then. Now why should I pretend that—

Harold: I'm not talking about the idea. I guess I'm talking about the climate.

Alicia: The climate! Now you've lost me. If people are so thin-skinned that a little reality shuts them down, then they're in the wrong business.

Harold: Well, I think it makes a difference. If you—

Alicia: We're in a race, you know? And I want the most from my people.

Harold: That's what I'm talking about. It's just that—

Alicia: *(defensive)* Oh, I get it. You know how to work with people and I don't, is that it?

Harold: No, no, no. It's not that at all. It's just that sometimes—

Alicia: Well, I think I've done just fine, thank you. But if you want to tell me how I should act . . .

Harold: Look, I didn't mean to overstep. I was only trying to help. Maybe I should have—

Alicia: See, I work with a certain kind of person. Our side of the business is a little more complicated than yours. It's a little faster and draws a more ambitious kind of person. I don't think you've ever worked in my area before, have you?

Harold finds himself in a pickle. Can he keep himself from becoming angry? That is perhaps his first test. Can he view the exchange impersonally even though Alicia feels so backed against the wall that she is making it personal? Can he create space for Alicia to expel her emotions, and then continue in a way that allows his personal regard for Alicia to come through? Or must he excuse himself and come back to the discussion later, when things have cooled down, pursuing his point of view and listening again to hers?

All of this depends on what Harold has made of himself as a person. Leaving the situation where it is, however, is to leave it unresolved. And unresolved issues fester.

Alicia seems on the verge of losing it. Again, we have no knowledge of Alicia or Harold prior to this scene. The "it" is her perspective, or—to put it another way—her objectivity, her ability to separate herself from her performance. Without "distance" from her performance, Alicia experiences Harold's critique as a critique of what she considers herself to be, and not of a performance that she can view objectively.

Alicia's challenge is the challenge we all face; namely, to evolve a commitment to our own growth to such an extent that we can hear and even welcome feedback on anything, feedback that we can then assess for its usefulness no matter how uncomfortable it makes us. If there is truth in the feedback, even if it is delivered poorly, we act on it. If there is no truth in the feedback, we do not act on it, but we do not dismiss it, either. Nor do we insulate ourselves from the prospect of further feedback. The task is to remain open, as required by both the Open-Mindedness Ethic and the Feedback Ethic. In the language of the previous paragraph, Alicia is unable to keep herself open because she perhaps identifies too strongly with her performance. If Alicia can shift some of her identity away from her performance and see herself rather as the *coordinator* of that performance, then the more mutable her performance becomes, something she *does* rather than something she *is*.

Perhaps this is an opportunity to pause for a moment and consider somewhat more deeply the notion of the self.[3]

For our purposes, there is value in suggesting that we are two selves throughout our lives, or perhaps, better to say, one self with two aspects: the observing self[4] and the created self.

The observing self is the awareness that develops in us very early in life, an awareness that looks out through our eyes and allows us to see the world from our point of view. This awareness develops gradually as the result of a thousand interactions and untold coaxing, through nurture and language. Eventually, however, it is there: an awareness of self, a capacity to "see" ourselves in the world, watching as we walk off to school, learn to ride a bike, drive a car—a capacity to witness ourselves. The observing self is sometimes considered the first self, the core self,[5] providing a locus point to which experience is connected throughout a lifetime, making possible *a continuity of consciousness*. It is the observing self that we refer to when we say that we feel we are the same as we have always been—the same person, ageless, timeless.[6]

The created self, on the other hand, is the self that can be observed, the self that is witnessed by both the observing self *and* by others. It is the self that operates in the world and that possesses a multifaceted repertoire that grows as the years go by. A repertoire shaped by the environment and, increasingly by choice. It is the created self to whom we refer when we say "I am that"—meaning, for example, I am a father, a brother, a blue-collar worker, a baseball player, a man of many interests. We are that, though "that" is ever changing, not the same today as yesterday and different again tomorrow.

And that is true: we are *that*, the created self, the ever-changing outcome of all our interactions. But we are also the observing self, a seemingly timeless awareness with our point of view. We are two selves: the one that behaves or performs and the one that observes, the work of art (or the "piece of work!") and the witness.

One self with two aspects: *Being and becoming.*

The created self is on the side of becoming, of fitting in or standing out. Consuming, creating, living life across a lifetime of goals, disappointments, victories, apprehensions. The created self is immersed in the drama of everyday life. To identify with the created self is understandable, but to identify with it too strongly is to become partially unconscious, leaving behind the capacity to watch the unfolding drama without being pulled into it. To identify too strongly with the created self is to lose perspective.[7]

This is not to say that we do not or should not, at times, become fully absorbed in what we are doing, wrapped up in it entirely. There is joy in that, perhaps necessity. Excellence in performance may require it. But we should not lose sight of the fact that we are more than that, always able to step back and gain the perspective of the observing self, that aspect of ourselves that permits a degree of objectivity not available in the throes of an emergency or in the burst of creative expression.

The observing self "sees," and in seeing, permits us to experience ourselves as more than what is seen. If we are the roles we adopt, the stream of thoughts and emotions that emerge in us, the actions that flow from us—indeed, if we are all that constitutes the created self—we are also something more. For all these actions, emotions, thoughts can be observed. They are "objects" of a subject capable of witnessing them. To experience the witnessing on occasion.as well as the becoming can help to undercut the seriousness and sense of high stakes that is sometimes associated with the created self, since that self is not felt to be the end-all of who we are.

There is a presumption here, or perhaps a hypothesis: To identify completely with the role we are playing—whether that role is father, actor, singer, teacher, what have you—to identify completely with the created self, is to become slightly unconscious. And in the end, this damages our ability to fully embody and creatively express the requirements of that role. It leads to a "robotizing," a loss of suppleness and grace. It takes the play out of the role and leads to clumsiness in the face of the more nuanced and subtle requirements of whatever role we are in. In other words, to become unconscious in this way is to lose the opportunity for mastery, mastery of whatever role we wish to play and, eventually, mastery of the self. It is to lose the capacity for detachment within involvement,[8] a capacity—according to philosopher Bruce Wilshire—necessary for and characteristic of all art, including the art of life.

All of this brings us back to Harold and Alicia and the dilemma that each face (and that we all face), namely: whether we can accept the feedback we are receiving, accept it so that the feedback (however it is delivered) can be evaluated and acted upon if improvements or benefits are to be had. Or are we so identified with the behavior that is the focus of the feedback that to maintain our equilibrium, we must dismiss the feedback, avoid it, escape from it—anything to keep in place our current sense of self?

Alicia stands in for all of us on this issue, as does Harold in a slightly different way. Each is being tested on their commitment to feedback, but tested also on their sense of themselves, on their knowledge of who they consider themselves to be. We are not merely the role we are playing. We are that and more, both created self and observing self. And our inability to experience this fact (as the observing self permits) allows the passions of the moment to overtake us. We become, in those moments, less conscious, smaller than we really are. This is critical because often the feedback we receive is not only about the lack of skill or effectiveness in our conduct, but about the way in which we are confused, unconscious, robotic, impersonal—about our failure to be as large or as purposeful or as conscious as we otherwise might be. This feedback is about our enlightenment, where we exhibit it and where we do not, and it is the most important feedback we ever receive. And turning this feedback to our advantage is one of the most important things we ever do.

> *"I hate exchanges like this one – you wind up thinking about it all day. Alicia is rude to Harold and to the person they were talking about. Harold offers feedback and is punished for it. The exchange ends abruptly. Where does it go from there. For me, this script drives home the importance of resolving issues as soon as possible after they arise. They fester otherwise. The cost to your equanimity is too great."*

> *"What about Harold? Maybe he should have said: 'Don't talk to me that way! I'm trying to help.' He seemed to back off... apologize... For what? It's hard to know what he should have done. On the other hand, what justification is there for Alicia to respond as she did?"*

> *"The point we're discussing—am I wrong about this—concerns a person's openness to feedback no matter how it is delivered. Whether you can take the truth in the feedback, if there is any, and use it to your advantage. Right?"*

—Participant comments
Ethics of Human Development Training Program

Scene 6: *Choice and Awareness*

A manager is reporting to his team about a meeting he just had with fellow managers.

Harry: They're giving me all kinds of grief! I'm talking about the other division heads. It sounds like they're kidding, but it's more than that. They're talking about how we're behind on what we promised, about how we're not going to make our quota. They know it's not our fault entirely, but they're serious. I hate going to those meetings. Puts me in a bad position. I know what to say, don't get me wrong. Still, past all that kidding, they're saying that we're not holding up our end! I know they're concerned. I'm concerned. It's not good . . .

Ben: (sitting silently)

Harry's remarks continue, characterized by concern, resentment, and a touch of anger. Team members listen intently—all except Ben who, though listening, is also witnessing his decision to not get involved. He stops himself from asking what is usually on the tip of his tongue: *How can we make this better? How can we solve this problem?* By that decision, that choice—whether he is aware of it or not—Ben removes himself however slightly from the organization.

Ben's stance may change. He may choose to get involved, perhaps try to solve the problem. But if not, if instead he chooses to stop himself again and again from (in effect) asking how the problem might be solved, he will remove himself even further from the organization. Taken to the extreme, if Ben continues to make this choice, he is likely to be confronted, perhaps even asked to leave. The irony is that if Ben is unwilling to acknowledge the way in which his own choices have removed him from the organization, he might exclaim, "How dare they! How dare they ask me to leave!" when in truth, Ben had been choosing not to be there for some time.

Is this too harsh? Unfair? Is Ben in fact responsible for his exit from the organization? Let us for the moment presume so... and if so, let us presume further that this situation might serve as a turning point in Ben's life.

If Ben can acknowledge to himself his role in removing himself from the organization, then he will take a meaningful step in the direction of his own agency as a person, a step away from his view of himself as a victim. This is his challenge: To recognize that we sometimes "do it to ourselves," that we sometimes create or participate in creating the negative events that come our way. Whatever Ben does with his experience, whatever he concludes, it is worth considering that his situation mirrors what many of us do to ourselves more often than we may want to acknowledge.

Consider, for example, how relationships sometimes end. Alice announces to Ted that their relationship is not working, perhaps has not worked for some time. Ted responds by saying: "It's not my fault! What about you?" but does not choose to ask—in fact, consciously stops himself from asking: "How can we make this better? What do we have to do?" This goes on for months, even years. Still, Ted chooses not to address the issue, preferring argument or withdrawal. Eventually, Alice asks Ted to leave when, in a very meaningful sense, Ted left long ago. Again, as with Ben, if choices are not acknowledged, if there is the pretense that choice is not involved, then

Ted may scream, "How dare she! She is responsible for this disaster, not me!" when, in fact, Ted played his part and more in creating the outcome.

Whether in the workplace or in private life, this is the Free Choice Ethic calling on us to live a life wherein, increasingly, we take responsibility for the quality of our involvements. The above examples have been stripped of the complexity that necessarily accompanies the ending of a relationship, whether with one's workplace or personal life. But the core of the issue comes down to the choices we make, choices that may go by quickly but that leave their mark.

Is the outcome that befalls Ben largely, perhaps entirely, self-caused, a result of his choice to not be involved? Though he comes to work each day, from the organization's point of view, he is rarely there! Does Ben want to leave the organization? Does Ted want to leave the relationship? Were both without the courage or conviction to own up to what they were choosing, so much so that they were willing (in effect) to make someone else act on behalf of what they themselves wanted?

This is a hard line of inquiry, but it is the inquiry required by the Free Choice Ethic, *the purpose of which is to push awareness down into the fine grain of give-and-take between self and world, to make fully conscious and one's own what was perhaps previously unconscious or denied.* This can be a very difficult, even painful process, a process of excavation and reconstruction as denial, hardened habits, destructive tendencies are unearthed and examined, their hold over us wrestled free as we will ourselves more often in the direction of our values. Freedom and responsibility are expanded in this way.

"Which ship goes oftenest on the rocks or to the bottom?" asks Don Juan rhetorically in George Bernard Shaw's "Don Juan in Hell." "The drifting ship or the ship with a pilot on board?"[9] The answer, of course, is that the drifting ship goes oftenest on the rocks. Drifting or otherwise refusing to take responsibility for where we are heading permits past conditioning, the will of others, larger and perhaps indifferent forces to determine direction and outcome. With a pilot—an increasingly conscious and responsible pilot—principles and current values can have their say.

Unless Bill and Ted recognize and take responsibility for the choices they are making, unless they stop denying that choice is involved, then they will prove themselves hard cases, questionable learners, likely to wind up in one situation after another of the sort described.

On the other hand, what Ben and Ted experienced are among the most important learning opportunities that ever come our way. If Ben and Ted can step back far enough to witness their own involvement in creating their unhappy circumstances, then they will substantially expand their awareness and hopefully gain a degree of responsibility they did not have before.

There are victims in this world; no denying that. We are not always, by any means, choosing or helping to create the outcomes that befall us. The above analysis is simply an effort to examine our own role, if any, in creating the "victimhood" we believe we experience. Certainly, the will of others and forces beyond our control have their say. And at any given moment, these other factors can affect our lives dramatically; affect for example the organizations and relationships of which we are a part, even whether our involvement is possible. But if it is possible, then the Free Choice Ethic offers a cautionary note—and a hopeful one, as well. It states that with respect to the organizations and relationships of which we are a part, we are involved by choice. No one is forcing us to be involved. We are choosing to be involved or choosing not to be involved. And by our choices, our decision-making and follow-through, we participate in the creation of our experience. Yes, there are many factors at play, from the personal to the societal, but the Free Choice Ethic insists that we nevertheless impose a high standard on ourselves: We have choice, and to an extent greater than we sometimes acknowledge, we craft and compose our lives. That is the view the Free Choice Ethic encourages us to embrace. By adherence to this view, we test and perhaps expand our ability to create. At the very least, we decrease the likelihood that we will conclude that we have been victimized by others when, upon close examination, we see that in some instances, quite possibly, we made choices that contributed to the unhappy situation in which we find ourselves.

> *"Behaving like you are being made or forced to do what you are doing is to keep your head down, your shoulders stooped, not literally but figuratively. You don't see possibility. Your feet are stuck. You just don't feel as free as when your head is up, back straight (again, I'm speaking figuratively), moving forward because you are choosing to do so. That's how it seems to me."*

> *"I saw someplace where Thomas Jefferson said, "Nothing is troublesome that we do willingly." I don't know if he said that or if it is true. It seems like I could come up with an argument against it if I tried. On the other hand, I do think there is truth in it. "I have to do the dishes" or "I have to mow the lawn" is different—a different experience altogether—than "I choose to wash the dishes" or "I choose to mow the lawn." You can say that you're just tricking yourself. It's the same trouble either way. But I don't think it is."*

—Participant comments
Ethics of Human Development Training Program

<u>Scene 7</u>: *The Wind Harp*

This script has five sections. Each section could occur over the course of a day or in rather rapid sequence. Each is between a supervisor and a supervisee.

Section 1 –

    Alex: Good morning, Lois. How are you this fine morning?

    Lois: Just great! How are you, Alex?

    Alex: Great! Say, Lois, if you've got a minute, I'd like to share with you what we've come up with as a solution to that scheduling problem we discussed the other day.

    Lois: Sure, Alex. I'd love to. Let me talk to Chris first, and then I'll be right with you.

Section 2 –

    Lois: Hi, Chris. Are you available?

    Chris: Available for what, Lois?

    Lois: To go over the revisions to our policies and procedures manual. I've drafted the changes, and we had talked about discussing them first thing this morning.

    Chris: Oh, right. Yes, I do want to go over them. I'm looking forward to it. Let me get with James for about five minutes and then we'll do it. And thanks in advance for your work on this.

Section 3 –

    Chris: Good morning, James. How are you?

    James: Come in and have a seat, Chris. Close the door if you would.

    Chris: Sure. What's up?

    James: I don't know what it's going to take, Chris. The performance of your department has been a disappointment to me. I'm wondering if the responsibility is too much, if maybe we ought to think about rearranging things.

    Chris: James, I don't understand. I thought everything was fine. You've never mentioned anything before.

    James: I'm very concerned at this point.

    Chris: Well, no, uh, yes, we'll work it out . . . whatever it takes. I had no idea. What can I do?

    James: I'm going to give that some thought. Right now, I'm late for a meeting. We'll meet later today or sometime tomorrow and figure out the best course of action.

Section 4 –

> Lois: Hi, Chris. Back from your meeting with James?
>
> Chris: Yep.
>
> Lois: OK. Well, here are the revisions. Pretty well done, if I do say so myself. As you can see—
>
> Chris: Did I say I was ready to do this?
>
> Lois: Well, no. I just thought that when you got back, we were going to—
>
> Chris: Well, you thought wrong. Why don't you use a little common courtesy and ask me if I'm ready to deal with this stuff? It's not exactly the most exciting reading we're talking about here.
>
> Lois: I know. I didn't say it was. I just thought—
>
> Chris: Look, Lois, I'll call you when I'm ready.

Section 5 --

> Alex: Just the person I was looking for. All set?
>
> Lois: All set for what?
>
> Alex: For the scheduling solution we came up with. I think you're going to like it.
>
> Lois: Alex, to tell you the truth, going over the scheduling issue is just about the last thing I want to do right now.
>
> Alex: Oh, I just thought—
>
> Lois: When the time is right, we'll deal with it. Understand?! And right now is not the time.
>
> Alex: Of course. It's just that—
>
> Lois: Look, Alex, use some judgment, would you?

The Wind Harp Ethic: *It is ethical to treat others as you would like to be treated even though you are not always so treated yourself; unethical not to find appropriate and safe avenues for the release of your anger, resentment, or rage.*

What the Wind Harp ethic prescribes is the opposite of what appears to be happening in sections 4 and 5 of this script. Chris takes the anger and resentment created by the way he was treated by James and turns them on Lois, who, in turn, turns them on Alex. And poor Alex—what does he do? Well, it depends. If he is as reactive as Chris and Lois, he may kick the dog, verbally abuse his spouse and children, or worse. As indicated in the discussion of the Wind Harp Ethic, this is the classic way in which organizational cultures become negative overnight; the way in which more anger is accumulated than can be managed or released safely.

James' management style is primitive. He raises a performance issue with Chris when there is no time for discussion. This is hardly enlightened leadership, though it does occur. The focus here, however, is on what Chris chooses to do in response to his treatment by James. Does he hold on to his feelings, process them as he readies himself for a later discussion with James? Or does he allow his feelings to overtake him, influencing how he will behave toward the next person in line?

He does the latter. And then Lois—the next person in line—does the same with Alex. Was there nothing else either of them could have done? Was Chris incapable of pausing for a moment, collecting his thoughts, perhaps letting Lois know that he had just been in a difficult meeting and now needed to spend his time differently? The same could be asked of Lois. We could also ask both Lois and Alex (and perhaps Chris): Was there no way for you to ask the person who was treating you rudely, "Is there something wrong? Is there something I can do?" or perhaps even, "If it's me, I know we can work it out. If it's not me, then maybe I can help." Is this too much to ask of us during interactions of this sort?

Our inability to behave in accord with the Wind Harp Ethic is the way in which we participate in, rather than interrupt, the spirit killing that goes on in families, organizations, and society. It is the way in which we damage, at least potentially, the morale, confidence, self-esteem, and drive of others. On the other hand, when we do not participate in this cycle of abuse, when we do not pass on to others the damage done to us, we perform a very important service. We leave others untouched by the negative and perhaps touched by the positive, moving them to consider that it is possible to remain conscious and purposeful even when offended or hurt.

In the above example, several individuals failed to stop themselves from passing their anger and resentment on to others. They were mistreated, but they did not address the mistreatment either in the moment or later, after having kept it to themselves. Instead, they passed the mistreatment on. The result, when they think about it—and they will think about it eventually—is that they will think less of themselves, both their morale and the morale of the organization diminished.

This dilemma invites us to manage our feelings, to not allow our negative feelings, however they have arisen, to take over and drive us to conduct we regret. At a deeper level, however, this dilemma invites us to enlarge our perspective, to expand it to the point that we do not take such experiences personally; a perspective that allows us right then and there to recognize that the behavior of the other person is not so much about us as it is about a frustration or a fear the other person cannot contain. To not take things personally, to not respond in such situations as though a personal affront has occurred, is an achievement of a high order. It necessarily implies the observing self, detachment within involvement, but it does not mean that we do not respond. It means that the full range of possible responses remains in play, our range of motion, our flexibility, our full repertoire not limited by our anger or resentment but, rather, available so that we can match the best and wisest that is in us to the requirements of a challenging situation.

"I think this is epidemic... people taking their anger or resentment out on others. It happens in the workplace, sure. But it happens everywhere. I presume that to some degree that's what's going on with bullies."

"Who is responsible for your behavior? The answer is obvious, isn't it? Otherwise, you're scapegoating. The devil made me do it! The boss made me do it. Wait a minute: The boss made you kick the dog or yell at your spouse? No, those are choices for which you are responsible. That's what I believe."

"For me, the script is about the cycle of violence in families, organizations, society at large. In situation after situation, we pass our anger and rage on to others and in so doing we impact their confidence, their self-esteem. Yes, I agree, its spirit killing. On the other hand, if you can keep from passing your anger and rage and mistreatment on to others, if you can keep from delivering to them what was delivered to you... Well, to me, there's beauty in that."

—Participant comments
Ethics of Human Development Training Program

"Seen in this way, history is the saga of the working out
of one's problems on others..."

—Ernest Becker
Escape From Evil

Scene 8: *Where Is Me?*

Here the scene shifts from the workplace to a busy downtown street. A homeless person approaches a passerby.

> Homeless person: Do you have any change? I sure could use it if you've got it to spare!

This is a common occurrence in many locales. It is an event about which many people have very strong feelings. There are too many variables at play to say exactly how one should respond. Homelessness, especially street homelessness, can be associated with drug and alcohol addiction, mental illness, domestic violence. There is a lack of employment in many communities, as well as a lack of affordable housing. At the same time, there are food banks, emergency shelters, transitional housing facilities, and charities to which one can give to address the problem. It's not clear at all how one should address this situation. An assessment in the very moment it occurs is required.

If there is aggression in the request, that is one thing; if there is not (as is presumed here), it is quite another. Someone wants something from us. We may or may not have it to give, and even if we do have it to give, we may not want to give it for any number of legitimate reasons.

In Zora Neale Hurston's novel *Their Eyes Were Watching God*, there is a passage pertinent to the above scene.[10] Hurston tells the story of Janie, a Black woman coming of age during the 1920s and 30s in Florida and Georgia. In her effort to recount her life, Janie tells a friend that she knew neither her mother nor her father and was raised by her grandmother, who she called Nanny because that's what the grandmother was called by the white children for whose parents Nanny worked.

Janie indicates that she had no idea she wasn't white until she was around six years old, as she only played and associated with white children. And, she adds, she wouldn't have learned it then had it not been for a group picture taken by a photographer passing through the area.

Janie recalls that in the picture, there was a very dark little girl standing where she was supposed to be standing. Janie did not recognize the little girl as herself, and so she asked: "Where is me?"

This is a poignant moment in the novel and a poignant question overall, perhaps the question at the heart of all philosophical inquiry. In a world so complex and seemingly indifferent, the sense of who one is can get confused, misplaced, lost altogether. Janie's question is a question we all ask from time to time. And if we do not have the support to help us understand where and who we are, we can find ourselves confused on this most fundamental of questions.

There are two points that may guide the passerby's response in the above scene. First, there is the notion that we are not entirely our situation, any more than we are entirely the self or person that is visible to others. To be sure, the homeless individual is in a difficult situation. It is a situation that may dominate his life, but it is not the "all of who he is". And to be treated as if we are only and entirely our situation can feel uncomfortable, perhaps disconcerting. In some cases, it can feel dishonoring. Nothing is more alienating than to be looked at but not seen, not recognized as a person behind whatever may lie on the surface. Even if our situation is not that of a homeless person but that of a wealthy landowner, an elected official, a star athlete, it can feel tiresome to always be treated as if you are only your role or station in life. Formalities exist. And based on the situation of the person in front of us, we may for many good reasons respond in accord with standard protocols. These protocols help us get through our everyday dealings with others. But it is important to remember that there is a human being behind and within any situation, *an observing self behind whatever mask is being worn.* Holding this fact in mind makes us a little less likely to act robotically or stereotypically when addressing others, more likely to have flexibility and care in our dealings with them.

The second point that may guide the passerby's response is this: The ability to look past the mask to the person wearing it is a measure of how well we know ourselves.[11] And we know ourselves best by carefully observing and examining our own lives, our everyday strivings, the ways we have triumphed, and the ways we have avoided life's challenges. To look carefully at our lives is to see how we have changed over time and what was required of us to bring about that change. It is also to see our resistance to change even when reason called for it. We observe our past and perhaps current inclination to escape and avoid, as well as our occasional forthrightness. And we see how far we may deviate on occasion from our espoused ideal. To see into our lives in this way is to know ourselves more completely, with fewer misconceptions and far less denial. It is to acquire self-knowledge, and with such knowledge comes the understanding of how selves, any self, all selves, are made. "Know thyself" and as we proceed with this requirement, our empathy for others increases.

To say of the homeless person (or anyone else for that matter), "I am nothing like him," is to offer too casual a response. The suggestion here is that as we come to know ourselves, we see how similar we are to others. Potent factors separate us, yes, the situation into which we were born, our genetic propensities, the parenting and schooling we received, all precede and influence our capacity for choice. We are not blank slates when we enter the world, and we do not start out at the same place. We develop at different rates and the obstacles we face vary. But we are all capable of developing, of acquiring greater degrees of responsibility and self-direction. This is true for most of us whatever our starting point and whatever our history. To the question "Where is me?" the answer is, "I am the person in front of me. And depending on how well I know myself, I see myself had things gone differently."

This response does not prescribe exactly what should be done in this situation. As indicated above, there are simply too many variables. The exact response must be determined in the moment, in the sequence of moments that constitute the situation, as is true of all the dilemmas we have considered, each with its complexity stripped away so core dynamics are visible and available for discussion. But it does increase the likelihood that the response, whatever it is, will have a greater degree of humanity in it, that it will have respect for self and other embedded in it, guiding the interaction through to its completion, though what is done may take many different forms. Conceptually, however, the issue is one of identity, knowing oneself to such an extent that we can see ourselves in others and others in ourselves. To the question, "Where is me?" the answer is: Everywhere, or if not everywhere, then as far as my moral imagination will permit me to see.[13]

"I don't know where to begin with this. This has happened to me more times than I can count. I guess this is what you mean about 'the question being posed'. First of all, the proper term is unhoused, not homeless. Right? On the other hand, I know you're talking about a condition... possible to feel homeless even though you are housed or employed. It's a horrible feeling. Yeah, it's about the role of luck in our lives... the danger of blaming others for their bad luck... taking credit for our good luck. It's a kind of confusion."

"Also, you come across people who say they don't believe in luck. That people should take responsibility for their lives. OK, fine. It's just that responsibility used to be spelled response-ability. Where do they think that ability came from? So many factors you had nothing to do with set you on the path that allowed you to acquire those abilities. Responsibility... sure, fine, but compassion, as well. The deeper analysis leads to compassion. That's what I think."

—Participant comments
Ethics of Human Development Training Program

<u>Scene 9</u>: *Lovers and Teachers*

An elderly woman, perhaps in her eighties, and her daughter meet at the mother's home.[13]

Daughter: Hi, Mom.

Mother: Hi, Honey.

Daughter: How are you, Mom? Are you doing OK?

Mother: Sure, great. Just great.

Daughter: It's a beautiful day.

Mother: Oh, it is, just a beautiful day. What did you do today, Honey?

Daughter: I had the most amazing day, Mom. I was given an award for my service to the community. It came as a complete surprise. The people at work arranged the whole thing. There was a formal presentation, people made speeches. I wish you could have been there. You would have been so proud of me.

Mother: That's wonderful, Honey, just wonderful.

[Extended pause.]

Daughter: So, Mom, what are you fixing for yourself?

Mother: Well, I'm not sure . . .

Daughter: You're not sure?

Mother: Honey, how do you fix an egg?

Daughter: You don't remember how to fix an egg? [Pause.] Well, let's see. I think I can help you with that.

Mother: Oh, that would be great.

Daughter: No problem at all, Mom.

Mother: It's a beautiful day, isn't it?

Daughter: It sure is . . .

Mother: What did you do today, Honey?

Daughter: Mom! The award! The people at work . . .

Mother: Oh, yeah. The award. Who got the award?

[Long pause.]

Daughter: Should we go for a walk, Mom?

Mother: That would be great.

Daughter: Margaret is coming this afternoon.

Mother: Margaret? Who is Margaret?

Daughter: She comes and spends the afternoon with you three days a week. You sing songs with her. You watch television, your favorite shows.

Mother: Do I like her?

Daughter: Yes, Mom, you're crazy about her. She's so nice.

Mother: I'd rather you stay. Can you stay? I don't want to be with a stranger.

Daughter: Margaret's not a stranger, Mom. She's part of our family now.

Mother: Oh.

Daughter: As soon as you see her, you'll remember. Margaret's a good person to spend time with.

[Pause.]

Mother: It's a beautiful day, don't you think?

What are we to do with the heartbreaking losses that come our way: the loss of a job, divorce, the death of a loved one? In the above script, the mother is suffering from dementia, and by this fact alone, she presents her daughter with multiple challenges. The daughter is likely struck with a deep sadness. There are conversations certain to go unfinished and loose ends never to be tied up.

The degree to which we are prepared for such losses varies considerably. In this case, an important relationship is changing. The daughter already feels the loss. Frustration, despair, even anger can result. And yet here, as with all ethical dilemmas, is opportunity (as wrong as that word may seem to the daughter).

Human potential author Ken Keyes suggested that it is sometimes helpful to consider the world populated with two kinds of people: lovers and teachers.[14] Lovers, he suggested, are those people who, through their interactions with us, introduce us to that "stuff" in ourselves (feelings, attitudes, abilities) that we love. Teachers, on the other hand, are those people who, through their interactions with us, introduce us to that stuff in ourselves that we do not love. Of course, some people do not affect us either way. And with any long-term relationship, the individual with whom we are involved is no doubt both lover and teacher. This is simply a conceptual tool. A way for turning our experience with others to our advantage.

It is not uncommon, for example, to hear people talk about how they dread the holidays with their family: "Because he makes me so upset!" "Because she drives me crazy!" It is a painful situation existing in many families, and one that can last for years until, perhaps, Keyes' conceptual tool (or something like it) is applied.

What is the desirable skill or behavior I am being invited to learn by my teacher, the skill that would allow me to be myself in their presence, without tension or anger? Perhaps it is the capacity to live and let live, to not take what is said personally, to say my truth forthrightly, to love unconditionally. To see the situation in those terms is to put the ball in our court.

Even in situations in which problems between us and others have become entrenched, the realization that they are also teachers, whatever else they are (father, mother, sibling, coworker, etc.), can be helpful. It doesn't matter that they are unconscious of their role as teacher or that they are employing "teaching methods" we deplore. They nevertheless are helping us identify the skills, attitudes, behaviors, etc., that, if acquired, expand the range of situations and settings in which we can operate as ourselves, at ease, with less avoidance, fear, or blame.

In the above scene, the daughter, armed with Keyes' tool or some version of it, asks: "What is my mother teaching me, or more exactly, what is she giving me the opportunity to learn?" It is the daughters to determine. Perhaps it is to be selfless to a degree she has never been before, acquiring the discipline and flexibility sufficient to ensure that continuous care is provided. To feel that as she is *giving,* she is *getting* as much or more in return. Perhaps to witness herself honoring a mother/daughter relationship in timeless, archetypic fashion. Not alone but supported by what others throughout time have done. Whatever the case, let us presume, the daughter sees a way of constructively, creatively, lovingly, answering the question that is being posed.

> *"I can identify. I was so tired of the long drive home after our Thanksgiving visit, talking to myself about the arguments. The anger. The lover-teacher thing helped. I think it gave me just enough distance or objectivity or something . . . I would almost laugh at myself, my inability to learn what I was being taught."*

> *"I think it's incredibly hard . . . changing to a new pattern. You get in the habit of interacting with someone in a destructive way, and you stay locked-in. You don't change. I sometimes think that what breaks you out of it is disgust. You get disgusted at yourself. That's how I stopped smoking. I just got disgusted with the hold it had over me."*

—Participant comments
Ethics of Human Development Training Program

<u>Scene 10</u>: *Purpose and Meaning*

Two old friends, movie lovers, on a walk.

Frank: Remember the film *'Round Midnight?* I think we saw it together.

Reggie: *Round Midnight?*

Frank: It took place in Paris. Two men: One a Frenchman, an "everyman" who loves American jazz. The other a great American jazz saxophonist. He's older than the Frenchman, maybe near the end of his life.

Reggie: Sorry. Doesn't ring a bell.

Frank: At one point, the jazz musician is sitting in a café with a woman with whom he was once close. He's sad, maybe depressed. The woman asks him what's wrong and he says he's not sure he has anything left to give.

Reggie: If he has anything left to give?

Frank: Even a great jazz musician can wonder about something like that.

Reggie: Something to contribute?

Frank: That's what he wondered. Seeing himself make a difference.

Reggie: Maybe he had given enough. Time for him to not worry about it.

Frank: The movie made me think that it's a lifelong concern. Feeling like you're playing a meaningful part. *Reciprocity.* That's the word I was looking for.

Reggie: Reciprocity.

Frank: Like, you and me. We've been given a pretty good life. So, what are we giving back? Maybe not now, but eventually. I'm thinking about myself when I ask that... But what's your answer? For the sake of discussion...

Reggie: I'm a teacher. You're a painter. But you've got students, too. We're always giving what we know to somebody, many somebodies, usually.

Frank: I know. But when we get older. Is that what we'll do? Maybe. I guess so. I just got the feeling from the movie, from the old jazz man, that the will to live is tied up with this idea. Contribute or lose your sense of purpose and meaning. And then, what's the point?

The Gift Sharing Ethic: *turning your experience to the benefit of others, at least one other.*

There is an assumption at the heart of the Gift Sharing Ethic that we have yet to consider. Perhaps it is so obvious it goes without saying: Our life is not ours alone. Nor is our history ours alone. Rather, we belong to one another. Each of us a part of a single enterprise to which we contribute in one way or another.

A problem arises when we come to believe, as we sometimes do, that we no longer belong and even if we do belong, we no longer have anything to contribute. Maybe Frank is right. Maybe when we feel that way the will to live weakens. Perhaps also the respect we have for ourselves and others. *If we do not belong here, why care, nurture, contribute, preserve, do no harm?* The Gift Sharing Ethic acknowledges our interdependency, our shared responsibility for the future by calling on us to contribute to others, at least one other... contribute what our history has allowed us to know and do. As Robin Wall Kimmerer writes in *Braiding Sweetgrass:* "All flourishing is mutual."[15]

> *"I think the use of the term "gift" can be misleading. We're really just talking about giving to others what life has taught us or has permitted us to know and do. I should add, giving it only if wanted. I don't know why I add that last thought. Maybe I'm thinking of the guy who insists on playing his guitar at the party."*

> *"Depression... I agree that one of the ways your spirit gets weakened or in some cases broken is through a lost sense of personal value. What's the point if you aren't of value to others? You didn't acquire all the experience and knowledge you acquired just for yourself. Maybe you did but I don't think so. I share the jazz musician's concern."*

> *"I knew a serious-minded fellow who survived harrowing combat experiences and when we would talk philosophy, he would always say: "I'm here to serve." I respected that. The guy would help you out... his family and friends, but complete strangers, as well. His duty, he said."*

> *"John Dewey, the philosopher... I saw where he wrote: "So act as to increase the meaning of present experience." (Conduct and Morals) That's what Frank was talking about, don't you think? If you can contribute to others, then you are, most likely, increasing the meaning of present experience.*

—Participant comments
Ethics of Human Development Training Program

<u>Scene 11</u>: *Realization and the Ongoing Dialogue*

Two brothers are engaged in conversation as they sit on a porch overlooking the countryside.

Murray:　I figured it out!

Arnold:　You figured what out?

Murray:　The problem.

Arnold:　You figured out "the problem"?

Murray:　It came to me in a flash.

Arnold:　*THE problem!*

Murray:　Well, maybe not *the* problem, maybe just my problem.

Arnold:　*(kidding)* I didn't know you had a problem.

Murray:　*Really!*

Arnold:　On second thought.

Murray:　It's a relief in a way.

Arnold:　And what, dare I ask, is your problem?

Murray:　Well, I'll put it plainly: *I'm in shock... for some time now. Shock.* It's the only thing I can think of to account for it.

Arnold:　To account for what?

Murray:　For the way I've been.

Arnold:　And how have you been, if I may ask?

Murray:　*(half laughing)* Please!

Arnold:　Shock, huh? And what is responsible for this shock of yours?

Murray:　You name it.

Arnold:　Oh, come on!

Murray:　No, really. You name it!

Arnold:　*(sarcastically) Being born!*

Murray:　Yes, maybe! Or when I was bullied. When I was made fun of... called ugly.

Arnold:　You've got to be kidding!

Murray: Being rejected by Regina Reynolds in the fifth grade... Having to fight other kids. The death of our parents.

Arnold: Everyone goes through these things. It's just a part of life.

Murray: When I saw how much some people have and how some people have nothing!

Arnold: *(losing patience)* You're kidding, right?

Murray: These are shocking events, Arnold, shocking things to experience.

Arnold: Life has you in shock!

Murray: And furthermore—forgive me, old boy, but I see it in you, as well.

Arnold: Oh, come on... Everyone in shock?

Murray: Well, maybe not everyone.

Arnold: *(sarcastically)* The whole world in shock!

Murray: No, not everyone. But these things are shocking . . . blows to the nervous system. Some part of us shuts down when they happen to us.

Arnold: Is this your effort to come up with an excuse for being a jerk? "Excuse me, Madam, I can't help it. I'm in shock!"

Murray: No. It's not.

Arnold: Then what's the point?

Murray: I'm just saying that a lot of shocking things happen to us. Even the things you say are "just a part of life." They're shocking. Like when you get shamed in front of other people, or when you realize—I mean really realize—that everyone you love is going to die.

Arnold: How about them Lakers!

Murray: You know what I'm saying.

Arnold: Maybe, but this is—

Murray: For the sake of discussion, what am I saying?

Arnold: *(reluctantly)* Well, Doctor, you're saying we're shocked by some of the things that happen to us, and we shut down.

Murray: Yes, exactly. We go unconscious. We become less vital, more absentminded.

Arnold: *(sarcastically)* We go unconscious—*really?*

Murray: And you're dealing with it, as well.

Arnold: It's just life, Murray!

Murray: Yes, it's just life.

Arnold: *(sarcastically)* Big deal!

Murray: I agree.

The challenges that confront these brothers are subtle. Murray has an insight. From the vantage point of this book, it doesn't matter if his insight is correct. It matters only that it may lead to a change in awareness or behavior that Murray finds useful. Life does give us insights. It yields gold if we seek it. And the Personal Growth Ethic states that we must seek it, that it is our responsibility to continue to grow as persons, to deepen our understanding of who we are and of how we got made, and to reflect that understanding in our behavior.

The challenge for Arnold is to remain open, especially given that Murray is suggesting that Arnold is also in shock. However absurd this notion seems to Arnold; it nevertheless is a notion that for Murray has merit. Can Arnold suspend his skepticism long enough to consider Murray's idea?

Arnold: Look, maybe you're on to something. I'm not saying you're not.

Murray: *(surprise)* You're giving in?

Arnold: I'm your brother. I don't give in.

Murray: I'm just saying that we get crusty and stiff. We back ourselves into the
same old routine. Our eyes glaze over.

Arnold: We're in shock?

Murray: We don't even know it. We get dulled by these shocking events, dulled
and disorganized.

Arnold: Maybe you're just describing yourself.

Murray: Yes, I'm describing myself.

Arnold: But that's not all you're saying.

Murray: No.

Arnold: You're saying it's also me.

Murray: Shock rings true to me, Arnold. I look around and everyone seems to have
a degree of it.

Arnold: Everyone?

Murray: No, I suppose some people show no sign of it.

Arnold: But most people?

Murray: I don't think I knew what I was working on, or thinking about, until this
idea hit me.

Arnold: You don't think you knew what you were thinking about? You *are* in
trouble!

Murray: I think I was trying to get to this idea, or some idea that would allow me
to understand why I am sometimes not present, *not fully here,* why I phase
in and out. I was noticing that about myself, and it was bothering me.

Arnold: This is crazy... *Are you here now?*

Murray: You're right, though.

Arnold: I'm right?

Murray: It's a matter of what we do with an idea like this.

Arnold: I'm not doing anything. It's your idea!

Once again, it doesn't matter if Murray's insight is in some sense correct. These are two brothers—
friends, as well—sitting on a porch and discussing life, looking into life. One of them thinks he
now knows more about himself than he knew before. He sees what previously he did not see. And
yet, what does insight matter if it does not lead to new choices, a new capacity for follow-through,
new ways of being in the world.

Arnold: Shock. You're in shock . . .

Murray: I've been coming out of it. That's what I think, enough, at least, to finally
see it.

Arnold: And the upshot...

Murray: I feel more aware of myself. I can do things I couldn't do before . . . at
least I think I can.

Arnold: So how did this so-called insight dawn on you?

Murray: Well, to be honest, I was looking in the mirror and I—

Arnold: The mirror?

Murray: Yes, the mirror. And for a moment, just a quick moment, I saw that I
wasn't all there.

Arnold: *(incredulous)* Well, if that's what you needed to know, I could have told
you that!

Murray: Dismiss it if you like, Arnold, but—

Arnold: I'm just asking, Murray. I have a responsibility—

Murray: I feel looser, that's the thing. Freer. Like I've taken off my uniform. I'm enjoying the—

Arnold: *(brotherly kidding)* So where do you go from here? *Is there a local institution?*

Murray: I think I need to take this extra energy I'm feeling and put it into what I care about.

Arnold: Come again?

Murray: You apply the understanding your insight gives you, the new range of motion it gives you, especially if you want more.

Arnold: And so it goes?

Murray: Yes, exactly. And so it goes.

Arnold: I have no idea why I said that.

Murray: We're just talking here, Arnold. Like we always do. It would seem nuts to me, too, if it hadn't hit me so hard. Our vitality dulled by the shocks of everyday life. That's what I'm saying has happened to me. To us. To so many of us.

Murray's insight is not about shock alone, but includes a way of proceeding, a way of traveling the Yellow Brick Road, though he doesn't put it that way. He offers his insight and then suggests that to honor the insight, he must act on it, test its value, put it to use. Murray argues for the Conscious Mistakes Ethic, the importance of living up to what he now knows or believes is true. *Align conduct with an ever-expanding consciousness... therein lies method for the realization of inherent possibilities.*

There is another ethic as well alluded to in the above exchange, though obliquely: the Sustainability Ethic. After the moment of insight and as we labor through conduct to explore its worth, we must find ways to sustain our effort. Dialogue is one of those ways. Dialogue with trusted friends, fellow travelers, individuals who understand in their own way and on their own terms the nature of the topic. These dialogues may be both playful and testing, but at base they force clarity where fuzziness exists and perspective when it is clear we have taken ourselves too seriously. They give us the ongoing opportunity to ask: *What is this, this thing we are in?* ...they give us the opportunity to ponder aloud the *Mystery*. Such dialogues address a deep hunger and, from the human logic point of view, are a form of wealth.

> *"I think it is very important to have someone in your life genuinely interested in you, someone who will stop you in mid-sentence and ask you what you mean. You're on the road, right? You're driving. Your pal is in the passenger's seat looking out the same windshield. You say: "Look at that!" And your pal responds: "I can't see it." Or "That's not what you think it is." Or "I would have missed it.*

Thanks!" It's helpful to have someone willing to help you clarify what you're seeing and someone who is willing to point out what you might be missing."

—Participant comment
Ethics of Human Development Training Program

SUMMARY

To say that life is a morality play is to say, simply, that life is populated with challenges, ethical dilemmas, large and small, and that how we choose to behave in response to these dilemmas has developmental implications for us and for the society and culture of which we are a part.

Our task is to detect these dilemmas, to recognize when *the question is being posed,* and then, to address them as ethically as possible. By our effort, we are grown (in the Five Levels sense). Providing we persist, learning as we go, course-correcting, as needed, we acquire a moral or ethical sturdiness that renders us less often deterred by fear, more able to manage and enjoy the freedom we are securing for ourselves. More able to remain conscious—as opposed to shutting down.

Part III provided dilemmas that address central themes (choice, for example, or continuous personal development), but the examples used to illustrate these themes could have varied considerably. In one scene, anger and resentment are passed from one person to the next in a work setting, but the issue or problem is common to society at large. In another scene, a daughter deals with the loss of her mother, but loss visits everyone and takes many forms. While we may not have experienced any of the examples as illustrated, everyday life is certain to send us variations on these themes.

We turn now to a consideration of three topics, two that aid us in the realization of inherent possibilities, one that illustrates the way in which our behavioral/ethical development benefits others.

Part IV

Consciousness, Valued Behavior
& the Center of Gravity

"And if quality of consciousness matters, then anything that alters consciousness in the direction of unselfishness, objectivity, and realism is to be connected with virtue."[1]

—Iris Murdoch
The Sovereignty of Good

Part IV introduces three topics, two constitute strategies for the management of the self and one connects the individual to the larger context of which the individual is a part.

Before proceeding with the first of these topics, the topic of consciousness, it might be useful to pause here and acknowledge an assumption operating throughout this book. The assumption is this: The moment-to-moment exchange between person and environment is made of three parts. There is the moment as we find it, *consisting in part of our consciousness, of what we have in mind.* There is the behavior we engage in. And there are the consequences that follow. What we have in mind exerts its influence (along with other factors) and then is influenced by the consequences that result from what we do.

It is this ongoing interaction with the environment that makes us who we are. And our consciousness, what we have in mind, our *mindset,* is one element in this interaction.

GIFT AND ACHIEVEMENT

Consciousness is both gift and achievement. Gift courtesy of evolution and achievement courtesy of our own efforts.

From the evolutionary point of view, we are the species that found advantage in becoming increasingly self-aware, increasingly aware, as well, of the environment in which we operate. Advantage also in being able to communicate this awareness, this *knowing,* to others. The survival imperative gave us a hunger for knowing, a hunger also for what we might become... the realization of inherent possibilities. Thus, we are born ready to be made conscious. An embodied complex nervous system with the capacity to act in multiple ways on the environment, and to imagine (and be curious about) what will happen when we do.

One's own consciousness, however, though made possible by evolution is at some point ours for the making. The quality of our consciousness, to use Murdoch's phrase, is shaped by our choices—by what we attend to, the principles to which we adhere, the behavior we engage in. We cultivate our consciousness, heightening, deepening, expanding it by our decisions to do so and by the experience (the consequences) that follows. It is remarkable the variation in individual consciousness and staggering the height and breadth to which some people seem to have taken it.

Thus, in brief, the *phylogeny* and *ontogeny* of consciousness, the long evolution of a remarkable species, and the development of the increasingly conscious individual (the Five Levels an ontological sequence).

With consciousness, the key question is: Consciousness of what? According to Howard Rachlin, in his book *Escape of the Mind,* "...consciousness always seems to have an object. ...consciousness is always consciousness *of* something."[2] That "something" can include not only objects and activities in the world but our own thinking and imagining, the ideas and values to which we attend.

The point here, alluded to in Murdoch's quote, is that consciousness matters because *what we are conscious of is part of the environment we are in, the environment that calls on us to act and then affects—along with our personal history—what we are likely to do.* The person whose mind is filled with thoughts of their own worthlessness or the worthlessness of others or who is to blame is in a very different environment then is the person whose mind is focused on their values, goals, and dreams.

THE IDEAS AND VALUES TO WHICH WE ATTEND

In *The Sovereignty of Good,* Iris Murdoch writes: "It is... a psychological fact, and one of importance in moral philosophy, that we can all receive moral help by focusing our attention upon things which are valuable: virtuous people, great art, perhaps...the idea of goodness itself. ...There is nothing odd or mystical about this, or about the fact that our ability to act well 'when the time comes' depends partly, perhaps largely, upon the quality of our habitual objects of attention."[3]

Economist E. F. Schumacher makes the same point in his book *A Guide for the Perplexed.* "Our circumstances are not merely the facts of life as we meet them, but also, and even more, the ideas in our minds. It is impossible to obtain any control over circumstances without first obtaining control over the ideas in one's mind."[4]

Yoga, he writes, ". . . is [about] the control of the ideas in the mind."[5] Schumacher argues that yoga, meditation, and continuous inner prayer are all techniques for obtaining control over the ideas held in mind, whatever else their purpose.

To these techniques should be added the many techniques developed by modern psychology to accomplish the same end.[6] Techniques in service to the observing self, techniques and methods that permit the witnessing of mental life and, through that witnessing, to realize that we are not one and the same with it, and that mental life can change, can *be* changed.

Life coaching systems, for example, employ methodologies for keeping one's values, or perhaps one's vision or goal, in mind. Techniques for calling to mind as choice points arrive the values the individual would most like to have expressed in her behavior.[7] These techniques do not guarantee that the practitioner's behavior will express the intended value(s). Mindset is only one part of the equation. But they are an explicit recognition of the notion that what we have in mind the moment we are called on to act can be consequential.

One purpose of the *Mindfulness* movement, if it can be called that, is to quiet the mind, to see its activity, the objects of our attention, perhaps our "wrong-headedness", and then, increasingly, to think more clearly about life and how best to live it. To detect mental activity that pulls one astray, returning sooner to a mindset supportive of the activity and experience one desires.

Twelve-step programs help participants change their mind by encouraging them to memorize and recite as often as necessary the prayer of the twelve-step program. A new set of "ideas-in-mind" replacing less helpful thoughts and ideas, perhaps making less likely the next drink when the urges or next opportunity arrives. (The individual may drink. She may fall off the wagon.

But she now has a mindset—in addition to a support system—that encourages a break with the established pattern.)

The point is a simple one, perhaps obvious; namely, you can change your mind, the focus of your attention, your consciousness. And in the changing, make ethical conduct more likely. Entire traditions—whether religious, philosophical, or otherwise—have this as a basic assumption and goal. The ethics of human development are served by a mindset in support of them. A priming of the pump or a setting of the occasion. We can behave at odds with what we say we value. Fear or other factors can control the moment. But we exert in advance our preference for how we will behave by cultivating a consciousness that puts our values top of mind. This is part of what it means to be self-directing.

One last point. The cultivation of consciousness as just discussed is akin to the cultivation of wisdom. Ethical conduct made more likely and regret and bitterness made less likely. How else is wisdom to be measured? To the many arts we might practice in our pursuit of inherent possibilities, we are wise to add the art of putting in mind (focusing on) as continuously as needed the ideas, concepts, and values we would have guide us as we operate in the world.

PAIN, SUFFERING, AND VALUED BEHAVIOR

A discussion of ethics—of the art of life, in general—necessarily concerns the way in which our lives can come to be governed by escape and avoidance. We do not wish to suffer pain, anxiety, or discomfort, and so we avoid situations that in the past have been associated with those experiences. This makes perfect sense. This is what we should do except in those cases where the pain, anxiety, and discomfort stand between us and the realization of what we can become, between us and our dreams, goals, and developmental possibilities.

Pain and suffering, we should acknowledge, are an inevitable part of life.[8] They come to us by virtue of the fact that we are conscious of our own very limited and fragile existence. We have highly sensitive nervous systems that allow us to feel deeply, to register the slightest loss, and to anticipate and even dread what we fear is coming our way. We are certain to lose loved ones; certain to see those we care about suffer; certain to lose our youth, our innocence, our physical capacity; certain, that is, if we are fortunate enough to live a full lifetime. There is illness and infirmity, and there is injustice, the enormous disparities in this world that we cannot view directly without discomfort. Pain, loss, and suffering are an inevitable part of life, but we need not add to them unnecessarily. That is the point here.

Psychologist Steven Hayes defines valued behavior[9] as behavior consistent with our dreams and aspirations, in accord with our values and principles. From the point of view of this book, it is behavior that furthers our development as persons.

Hayes provides the following: *As we proceed with valued behavior, we discover that it necessarily induces a larger context within which to place our experience, including our suffering—a context that, because of what we have achieved through valued pursuits, also includes joy, the sense of accomplishment, feelings of fulfillment. We do not eliminate pain and suffering as we continue to engage in valued behavior. Nor are they denied or ignored. Rather, we place them in a wider context that allows us to see them and experience them as a part of, but not the whole of life.[10]*

This is the Pain-Directed Ethic, perhaps an enlarged understanding of it. We deal with the pain and suffering in our lives not by ignoring them or avoiding them, but by addressing them. And one of the ways we address them is by continuing to behave in accord with what we believe to be required for our continued development as persons. *We deal with them by continuing to engage in valued behavior.*

It is, of course, difficult to always behave in accord with one's values, especially when our fears encourage us to withdraw or retreat. And it is only with some hesitancy that any course of action can be recommended as some people have had to endure enormous pain and suffering. Who are we to say? And yet, this is the course argued for here because it marks the route that makes it less likely that we will add to our suffering unnecessarily. And further, because it is the route that will allow us to find whatever joy and fulfillment is ours to obtain. It is ethical to proceed with valued behavior—our duty to ourselves and to others—and to do so even though stress and suffering may be involved. Trust and resolve also are involved. And for some people, because of what they have had to endure already or may endure, something approaching the heroic is also involved.

Hayes discusses the pursuit of valued behavior by means of the following analogy: "You've been driving a bus called 'your life,' and along the way, you've picked up passengers . . . some you like, some you do not like. These are your memories, bodily sensations, conditioned emotions, programmed thoughts, historically produced urges, and so on." You've picked up a lifetime of experiences and these experiences "speak to you," they have voices, they are "on the bus." At every fork in the road, each has an opinion. Some may be screaming to stop or go forward, to take this turn and not that one; but as Hayes points out, they are passengers. You are driving the bus, and you have a very important decision to make: *to choose to drive in the direction of your values, the things you say you stand for, to drive in the direction of your own development as a person, or to drive in the direction that will allow some of your passengers to avoid their fears.* The former, writes Hayes, is "the path of vulnerability and risk, but it is about something... There is a distinction," he continues, "between you, the conscious driver of the bus, and the passengers you carry. You have room on the bus for them. You accept them. You defuse from them.[11] But then you turn your eyes back to the road and connect with that which you really value. You drive in that direction. As a result, your life grows a little, and it becomes a little more vital and flexible."[12]

We all have histories. And by the time we wake up and become aware of how our individual history has affected us, we can find that we have acquired an approach to life that is as much about escape and avoidance as it is about our values, aspirations, and goals. For too long, perhaps, we have allowed the passengers to steer the bus. And maybe this continues until we realize that living in pursuit of what we do not truly value is more painful than is the pain we experience when pursuing a life anchored to those values.

So, the cultivation of consciousness and the pursuit of valued behavior... strategies for bringing us into contact with and strengthening us to deal with the challenges that stand between us and the realization of our inherent possibilities. Self-making strategies. If embraced, a byproduct, perhaps offering motivation of its own, is the benefit these strategies provide others, some of whom we may never see or touch directly.

This is the last point for consideration in Part IV: how the ethical resolution of the dilemmas that come our way or the pursuit of valued behavior, in general, reaches beyond those with whom we are involved directly—not magically, but because we are connected to one another in ways that are nearly obvious when we stop to think about it.

THE CENTER OF GRAVITY

Philosopher Ken Wilber defines the concept of a center of gravity as follows:

> "Every society has a certain center of gravity . . . around which the culture's ethics, norms, rules, and basic institutions are organized, and this center of gravity provides the basic cultural cohesion and social integration for that society.
>
> "This cultural center of gravity acts like a magnet on individual development. If you are below the average level, it tends to pull you up. If you try to go above it, it tends to pull you down. The cultural center of gravity acts as a pacer of development—a magnet—pulling you up to the average expectable level of consciousness development. Beyond that, you're on your own, and lots of luck, because now the magnet will try to drag you down."[13]

With this concept, the behavior of the individual is linked to the health and vitality of the culture overall. That is its elegance, and one of the reasons it is so useful.

For example, every organization—every family, team, workplace, local community—has a culture, and thus its own center of gravity. If we enter a workplace, let's say, with a performance standard below the standard already established, then the forces operating within that workplace—peer pressure, new employee orientation, staff training, etc.—will operate on us to raise our performance to the established standard sooner than would occur otherwise. The center of gravity, acting like a magnet, pulls us up.

On the other hand, if we enter that workplace with a performance standard above the established standard, then the forces at play—peer pressure, lack of support for high performance, resistances of one sort or another—will tend to pull us down. Though by our behavior we point the workplace in the direction it should evolve, we do so at some cost to our own energy since the center of gravity, acting like a magnet, drags us down. Figure 1 depicts the effect of the center of gravity on individual performance in a workplace or organization (or community or society).

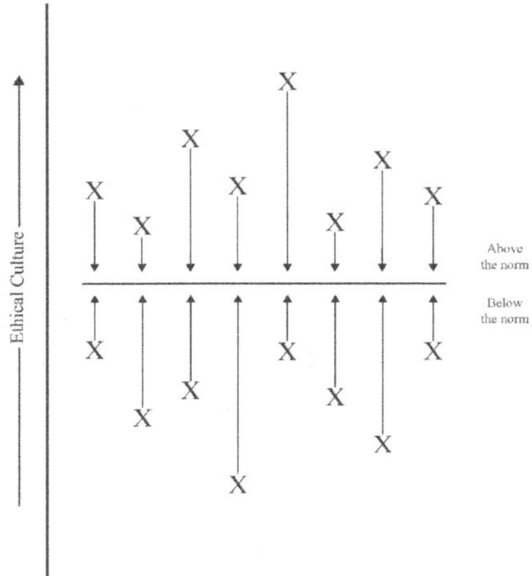

Figure 1 – Graphic depiction of an organization's center of gravity.
X's represent average performance levels of individuals
comprising the organization.

However, the reverse is also true: Just as the center of gravity exerts its effect on individual performance, so individual performance exerts its influence on the center of gravity. Other things being equal, when individual performance improves, the center of gravity rises. When individual performance declines, the center of gravity falls.

Figure 2 displays an organizational center of gravity that has risen over time as one or more individuals in the organization raise their performance level(s).

Now, suppose the organization depicted in Figure 2 is merely one of many such organizations in the community, all addressing the same issue (examples could include social service agencies working on homelessness or child abuse; departments within a large governmental agency; or businesses within the same industry, competitors on one level but collaborators when it comes to issues that affect the industry as a whole). Within this network of organizations, it is reasonable to assume that there exists a cultural center of gravity and that this center of gravity operates on and is responsive to organizational performance in the same way that the center of gravity within a single organization operates on and is responsive to individual performance.

If an organization enters this network operating below the network's established standard, then the forces operating within the network (i.e., collegial associations, established standards for products and services, accreditation processes, etc.) serve to raise the performance of that organization in the direction of the network standard sooner than would occur otherwise.

If, on the other hand, the organization enters the network operating above the network's standard, then it must maintain its higher standard largely on its own. Though by its performance it points the network in the direction of a higher standard, it does so at some cost to its resources as it is now using its energy in part to counter the pull of a lower standard.

Similarly, a community has a cultural center of gravity (as does society overall). Individual and organizational performance is affected in the same way that a network's center of gravity operates

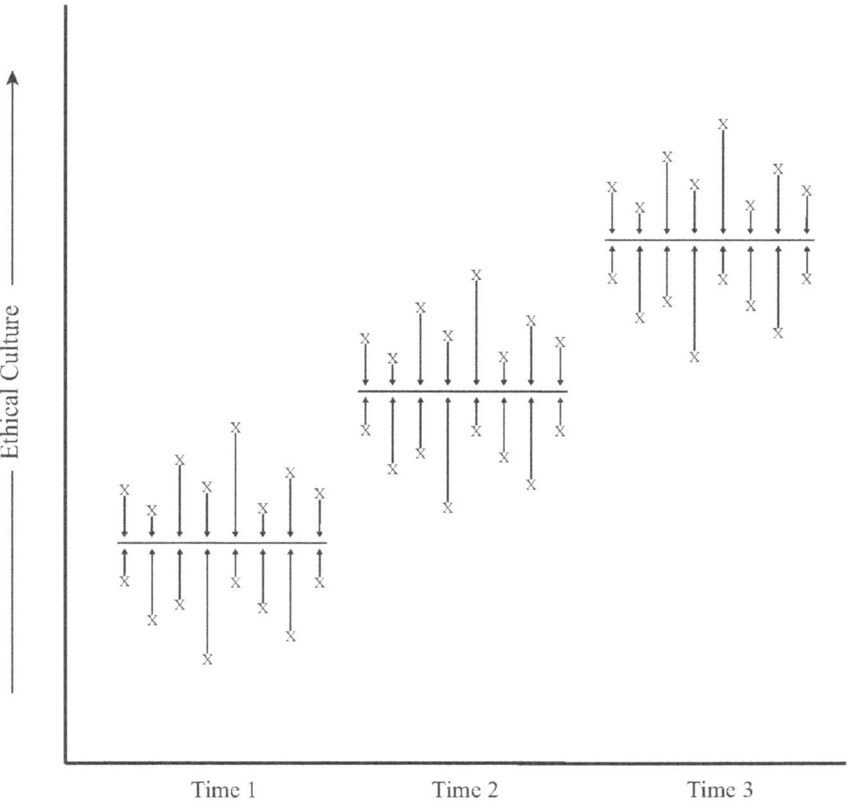

Figure 2 – Organizational center of gravity rising over time as one or more organizational members (X's) raise their performance level(s).

on organizational performance (and an organization's center of gravity operates on individual performance). Performance below the established standard is pulled up sooner than would occur otherwise. Performance above the established standard requires that the individual or organization rely more fully on motivations and supports interior to itself since the effect of the communitywide center of gravity is to drag down performance. High-performance may be appreciated—it may be a source of community pride—but the community's established standard does not support the higher standard and, over time, will tend to drag it down.

Thus, by means of their centers of gravity, organizations and communities exert their influence on their constituent parts; each part, in turn, exerting its influence on the evolving standard. Through our willingness to address the dilemmas that come our way, continuing with valued behavior despite the difficulty, we affect others, sometimes directly but also, by the above logic, through a standard we help establish.

Perhaps it would be appropriate to add that it is often very difficult to know the reach of any one ethically resolved dilemma or the impact of a consistently high standard of performance. Maybe the location of the cultural center of gravity (in family, workplace, or community) is not affected

125

in any discernable way. However, it is worth pointing out that when we witness or otherwise learn of an ethically resolved dilemma or of exceptional performance, even if the standard in the organization is yet to be affected, if at all, we frequently are moved. The part well played earns our admiration and may cause us to reflect on our own standard(s). We are emboldened by what we see is possible for others.

> (NOTE: With the center of gravity concept in mind, it is possible to expand what is typically thought of as the purpose of leadership. From the point of view of this book, the purpose of leadership is to raise the center of gravity. That is one of its duties. It is also one of the measures of good leadership. Whatever the organization (whether workplace, family, team, or society), the responsibility of leadership is to interact with the structures, components, processes, and individuals comprising the organization to raise the organization's center of gravity. However, it is not formal leadership's job alone. Whenever anyone in an organization behaves so as to raise the organization's center of gravity, leadership of a most fundamental sort is provided.)

SUMMARY

This book is about the difficult journey from childhood to whatever level of maturity is ours to obtain. It is about the journey of the self, a journey marked by the tests of heart and mind that serve as a measure of development.

The ideas we hold in mind, the ideas with which we see and meet the world, can aid us in the resolution of these tests. *Mindfulness*, the capacity to hold in mind the values we would have our behavior express. *Self-control*, the government of the self, the ability to engage in valued behavior even though our history and immediate environment may not support that behavior and may be at odds with it.

The ethics of human development provide guidance. They prescribe the standard and the conduct certain to educate, mature, and enlighten; certain eventually to have a beneficial impact on the center of gravity. Thus, we have argued, the ethics of human development, along with the ethical resolution of the dilemmas that come our way, are the means by which we travel the Yellow Brick Road.

Down that road, and with every step, lies the increase in ethical creativity. In other words, a maturity absent victimhood, bad faith, and the blaming of others, a maturity characterized increasingly by a willingness and desire to play what is called the non–zero sum game, a game wherein actions benefit not only us but also an ever-larger circle of others. The capacity to play this game is an inherent possibility, connecting self-interest to the development of others. And, importantly, the actual playing of the game is the life artist theme come back around, i.e., detachment within involvement; the pursuit of valued behavior; a self that can contain its entire history—its joy and its suffering—without that history deterring it from its purpose.

Part V

The Theater of Change

"It is an early spring evening in a semi-darkened warehouse in New York near the docks. The hour has passed at which Robert Whitman's theatre work 'Light Touch' was to have begun. People are still buying tickets . . .

"Awaiting the performance, we sat in the damp and gloom, uneasy over the continued delay . . .

"Then a strange event of disclosure occurred—a disclosure of disclosure. In the darkness, the main door of the warehouse in the middle of the wall before us slowly rolled up and opened. It went from floor to ceiling . . . the sounds of the city could be heard . . . and cars appeared occasionally, framed by the door, as they passed on the street directly outside. Appeared, but appeared transfigured, as if a spell had been cast over them. Details of their shape and movement, ordinarily not noticed leapt out . . . It was as if cars were being seen for the first time . . . The driver's intent gaze on the road in front of him chipped out merely a fragment of the world in which he moved.

"After a car had passed by in this side street, the space in which we were living would relax and expand again to admit the sounds of the vast city—Then again, as if we inhabited a breathing organism, events on the street would take prominence. Slowly and majestically, matters unleafed through time, yet also sadly, as if all of us—rapt and silent inside the warehouse—were aware that the spell that had been cast was fragile. One felt grateful to be alive and conscious."[1]

—Bruce Wilshire
Role Playing and Identity

In Part V, the training program created to teach the ethics of human development is discussed but only briefly... training methods and the rationale for those methods. The primary focus of Part V is on the philosophy behind the program, the emphasis on—the importance of—ethical development in us and in our organizations if we are to secure a future friendly to our collective wellbeing.

THE ETHICS OF HUMAN DEVELOPMENT TRAINING PROGRAM

Teaching ethics can be a sensitive matter. *"My ethics are just fine, thank you."* Room must be made within the training experience for each person to find their own way to the relevance of the material. Here are the basic assumptions shared with participants at the start of training:

Assumption #1: It's a healthy individual or heathy organization that invites this training; healthy enough to know that improvements are always possible, even when—especially when—it comes to ethical conduct.

Assumption #2: No one lives a totally ethical life; we all have improvements we could make. The training program is about the advantages that might accrue were we to make even slight improvements.

Assumption #3: To get the most out of the training, the emphasis throughout must be not on how others in our lives or in the organization are doing with respect to these ethics, but on "how I am doing"; the focus must be on oneself.

Assumption #4: The purpose of training is served best when participants feel safe, comfortable, their own current views honored; for this reason, participants are encouraged not to accept the ethics of human development uncritically, but to examine, discuss, and reflect on them, to treat them like a whetstone against which to sharpen and refine their own ethics if the ethics of human development prove inadequate to their needs.

The training components:

Presentation and discussion. Each ethic presented and discussed.

Image Theater. Exercises designed to bring the ethics and related concepts to life.

Role-playing. Scripts enacted depicting ethically challenging situations.

Workbook. Clarifying the personal/behavioral meaning of each ethic; determining one's own ethical conduct objectives.

The image theater component draws on the work of Brazilian theatrical scholar August Boal[2] and American family therapist Virginia Satir.[3] Both have pioneered the image theater concept, documenting its power to reveal and inspire.

The role-playing component[4] is comprised of scripted scenes enacted by two or more volunteer participants. Each scene reveals the absence of one or more of the ethics of human development (several of which were discussed in Part III),

When enacted, the role-playing scenes set the occasion for a useful and often clarifying discussion. However, the task is not simply to have a clarifying discussion—to have, for example, the missing ethic or ethics identified, and possible solutions discussed—but rather to have proposed solutions enacted in the scene. At various points in the discussion, participants are invited to take the place of one of the actors and to complete the scene in a way more in keeping with the ethics of human development. The result is practice in the difficult art of creating and improvising ethical solutions on the spot.

The image theater and role-playing exercises are built on the assumption that the most unforgettable and personally beneficial of all forms of theater is the theater in which we choose to act, the theater that addresses our problems and in which we (along with friends, colleagues, and coworkers) work to find a solution. The scripted scenes and the exercises that reveal the meaning of complex concepts invite participants to overcome their hesitancy and act on behalf of their own view and, by so doing, give themselves a hard-to-forget experience, one that they will review and perhaps mull over, enhancing their readiness to behave more effectively when similar situations arise in the future.

Participants also personalize the meaning of each ethic using the workbook. They identify and/or develop. individualized ethical conduct objectives. On occasion, a "One Week Report" is compiled and returned to the organization. This report lists the ethical conduct objectives undertaken and completed as of one-week following training.

Finally, at the end of training, participants complete a questionnaire rating their satisfaction with themselves and with the organization overall on ethics of human development measures. This information is turned into a report, an assessment of the ethical health of the organization. This report serves as baseline with the questionnaire administered on a periodic basis for the purpose of tracking progress.

THE THEATER OF CHANGE

One of the aims of the training program is akin to the theater piece described above. Figuratively speaking, the training program is an attempt "to raise the warehouse door," permitting participants to see the workplace or better, everyday life, the here and now, as the place wherein development occurs, or can occur depending on how we choose to behave.

Participants are encouraged to see themselves as actors in an ongoing play—not cogs in a machine but individuals capable of consciously and responsibly interacting with others and with organizational structures in ways that have developmental consequences. The aim, in other words, is to further participants' awareness of their capacity for choice, to make them aware of the fact that they are already engaged in choosing among many possibilities—hour by hour, minute by minute—however much they may have denied or been unaware of this fact previously.

This is one of the reasons role-players rehearse their scripts in advance. Participants generally enjoy seeing colleagues and friends enact a scene no matter how much they may stumble over a script, lose their place, fall out of character. But with rehearsal, the stumbling is minimized. Role-players give participants less to distract them from the opportunity for self-reflection.

As indicated in Part III, role-playing scenes and the training experience overall attempt *to help participants recognize when the question is being posed.* With every enacted scene, participants are asked: Is this scene relevant to you? Are there situations like it that occur in your everyday life? How about this scene? And this scene? The training experience, using many examples, attempts to help participants recognize those situations wherein the question is posed, and then to help them see themselves as capable of behaving in other ways if to do so seems desirable.

According to Wilshire, *theater* comes from the Greek word *theatron*, meaning "a place for seeing."[5] The training experience is an attempt to be such a place, a place where glimpses of the self can penetrate past defenses, giving participants a sharpened view of themselves and, in that "seeing," an awareness they did not have previously. In other words, to *see* and, in that seeing, to objectify, permitting examination and additional perspective, and if one does not like what is seen, to consider other ways of behaving.

A MEANS FOR SELF-MAKING

Ultimately, the focus of this book—and the training program designed to teach the ethics of human development—is on the making of the self. It is certainly true that we are inevitably and necessarily made or authored by others—fathers and mothers, teachers and peers, the social and moral order into which we are born. And these authoring influences are indispensable, so much so that without them, we might never acquire the ability to take over the task of self-making at the point where these influences leave off. We might never realize that it is our duty to continue working on a self that, by definition, others cannot finish for us. Hence, the reason and necessity for Ethic 11: *It is ethical to continue to grow as a person, to continue to increase your capacity to conduct yourself in accord with your ethics and principles; unethical to stop growing as a person.*

The point is that as the authoring goes on, the self increasingly becomes the product of its own making, not only taking over the task of self-making but taking responsibility for the self that has been made by others[6]—changing, undoing, modifying what others have shaped into being to the point that no one else, no other outside factor, is to be held responsible for who one is or how one behaves. Credit may be due to any number of influences, but blame is out of the equation. Increasingly, the individual, through his own efforts and having taken over the controls, has become a self-responsible agent. This is a tall order and difficult, but nevertheless a way of characterizing the far end of the developmental continuum discussed in Part I.

In *Role Playing and Identity*, Wilshire quotes the philosopher G. H. Mead: "The self arises in conduct."[7] We act our way to maturity by addressing the difficult situations that come our way. We learn from our mistakes, choosing and deciding and acting our way to a self that is socially responsible, able to join with others (or not join with others, as the case may be) in pursuit of interpersonal and social arrangements that are more creative and just.

One additional point: Self-making dilemmas, when met effectively, increase our belief in ourselves. They strengthen our willingness to persist despite the obstacles in front of us. A person cannot evolve without the willingness to persist. Arthur Schopenhauer, the nineteenth-century philosopher, defined the will as "the strong blind man who carries upon his shoulders the lame man who can see."[8] The training program prescribes a means—with its many role-playing and theater exercises—by which this blind man may be exercised and strengthened so that what is envisioned by the self for the self may be approximated through conduct.

FEAR AND LONGING

When individuals who have attended the training rate their satisfaction with their own performance and with the performance of the organization on ethics of human development measures, the items with which they invariably are least satisfied are: "eliminating escape and avoidance from the management of self and others," "the absence of procrastination," "acting decisively when the time to act has come," "providing feedback to others." Participants identify those items in which apprehension, anxiety, trepidation, or fear interfere with performance. Ethics training, therefore, is nearly as much about the way in which we are governed by fear as it is about the ethics that should characterize our behavior.

While the issue of fear is discussed throughout training, no one is asked to do anything they are uncomfortable doing. However, there is always the invitation to participate, the invitation to take greater risks, to enact and resolve the dilemma in each scene (the decision to do so a dilemma of its own). It is pointed out that the risking of oneself to enact one's best idea is rarely, if ever, a bad idea, especially in the protective context of training. At the very least, participation of that sort is a request for feedback and shaping. But it is something more, as well.

To get out of one's chair and attempt to enact a role-playing solution before an audience of both friends and new acquaintances, and to do so on behalf of an inkling or a conviction or an ideal is nothing less than a "turning of the Fool loose." It is using the play within the play for the cultivation of that very capacity that is needed both in the organization and in life—namely, the willingness to risk acting the fool on behalf of the best of what one knows, knowing that it may not be sufficient or the best of what can be known. Without this willingness, there is no evolution of self or society. And though the effort to do this by a given participant may appear clumsy or half-baked, such efforts are, in a sense, selfless. The individual stands in for others, modeling what it takes and, in the process, setting the occasion for the development of a culture that itself needs practice in supporting such behavior—practice at providing feedback and support for the very activity that will enliven it.

In *The Denial of Death,* Ernest Becker discusses what he calls "the neurotic type." Becker emphasizes the developmental value implicit in not sitting back but, instead, overcoming the fear— risking, acting, turning the Fool loose in small but meaningful ways for the cause of one's growth as a person. "The self arises in conduct," as Mead said. "To live," writes Becker, "is to engage in experience at least partly on the terms of the experience itself. One has to stick his neck out in the action without any guarantees about satisfaction or safety. One never knows how it will come out or how silly he will look, but the neurotic type wants these guarantees. He doesn't want to risk his self-image . . . Instead of living experience he (the neurotic) ideates it; instead of arranging it in action, he works it all out in his head".[9]

THE ROLE OF CULTURE

What is the role of culture in supporting ethical conduct and personal development? At base, culture is a framework of supports, of practices, of ways of giving and taking with others that become familiar and that allow for some degree of stability. And, as discussed previously, every culture has a center of gravity, defining the culture's ethical standard and then serving as both restraint and safety net. To perform above the center of gravity, to achieve and maintain an integrity not yet common in the culture, is one of the ways we serve others, helping to hold in place and perhaps raise the existing standard. To perform below the existing standard is to be drawn up... or, to be caught, a safety net, giving time for us to collect ourselves and fend off further disintegration.

Of the many things that a culture does, from the sense of place it offers its members to the flowering of the creative arts, one of its key features is that it serves as platform for individual development, milieu within which self-making and further integration can occur.

> (NOTE: Before going further, we should acknowledge that not all cultures are
> equal. While all provide frameworks, each with its center of gravity, it can hardly
> be said that all readily serve as platforms for further development or that all fend
> off disintegration. Some, it would seem, hasten it. There is gang culture, for
> example, the culture of organized crime; the enabling culture; cultures that are

racist, xenophobic, oppressive. And while these cultures exist because they serve some need—from the need to belong to the need to survive—still it can be argued that they are born out of external conditions that are themselves distorted: extreme poverty, inequality, powerlessness, conditions that often make for ill-formed and unprepared personalities, conditions that result in cultures with a limited ability to serve the long-term interests of their members. Here, however, as from the beginning of this book, the interest is in the development of cultures that do serve the long-term developmental interest of the individual, cultures that support and do not damage the individual's pursuit of inherent possibilities.)

There is another role culture can play in personal development. It is the role culture plays when used intentionally by individuals who recognize the power of culture to affect change. Most of us are a part of several organizations and, thus, several cultures at any one time. By taking responsibility for the cultures of which we are a part, we use the power of culture to accelerate development. By choosing wisely the community in which we live (if that option exists); by choosing carefully our friendships, our workplace; by inserting ourselves into cultures that educate us, keep us fit, encourage us to contribute to others—cultures that require us to exercise our flexibility, our creativity, cultures comprised of those we admire and that, in turn, require the best of us—by these means we create a "funnel of becoming."[10] Our affiliations, whether to individuals or organizations, can provide support for the further integration and wholeness that is possible for us. The goal remains progress on the Yellow Brick Road. But the pursuit of that goal can include this additional stratagem, the conscious use of culture—of many cultures patchworked together—to draw, pull, funnel, and support, accelerating the emergence of a human being that is creative, playful, principled, and compassionate. This achievement, if it does occur, belongs to the individual who accomplishes it but also to culture with its power to transform and refine.

Remember, as the term is used here, culture exists not only on a global, regional, and ethnic level but also in a neighborhood, a school, a classroom. A culture exists in every organization and workplace, in families, even between two people. The emphasis here is on the pattern of exchange between people, the give-and-take, and the values that pattern of exchange expresses and supports, rather than on the language, arts, and traditions of a given group. The point is to seek out and insert oneself into a pattern of exchange that is growth-promoting; the conscious, intentional use of culture to help bring about personal development, the refinement of self. To be clear, however, in this context refined means *soulful,* not sophistication in the world of arts and letters.

THE MORAL CLIMAX

As early as the 1970s, Buckminster Fuller argued that humanity is facing its final exam. Utopia or oblivion is the way he put it, the explosions in population, knowledge, interdependency, and awareness having driven humanity to this point.[11] Human beings cannot turn around now without bumping into one another. We are connected by proximity, though not by proximity alone. The planet is wired. Even in the most remote villages there are satellite dishes and, with them, awareness of the events, lifestyles, and disparities that characterize our historical moment. Furthermore, this planetary web only continues to tighten— interpersonally, organizationally, internationally—the result being that we just can't get away with wronging others as we used to. No longer is it as possible to "do unto others" without also "doing unto ourselves," to "win" at the expense of others without also experiencing some degree of loss.

To put it another way, we seem to be invited as never before by the potentially irreversible consequences of our actions to become more conscious, more responsible, more ethical, for our own sake if not for the sake of others. A more mature version of ourselves would appear to be needed, a version capable of considering the long-term consequences of actions and thus of aligning our actions with what is likely to work for more of us—ideally, for all of us—over the long run.

The question that must be answered and that resides at the heart of Fuller's "final exam" *and at the heart of this book*—unasked so far but in effect answered by how we respond to the dilemma he poses—is among the most fundamental questions that can be asked: *Who are we? What are we?* From the point of view of this book, the answer is: *We are the effects we have on others.*[12]

We may be more than that, but we are at least that. And while it is true that we can never know the exact or full effect we have on others, still, with detachment from our need for self-protective conclusions, we nevertheless can see that we are producing effects through our involvements with others and with the physical and biological environment—effects that may or may not be short-lived, that flow into and merge with the effects of others, but effects nonetheless.

As individuals who wish to evolve, it is our job to see these effects, to discern them however they trace through, contribute to, and condition the experience and development of others. In the seeing of these effects, we see ourselves. In our effects on others and on the physical and biological environment, we find the looking glass. And again, if what is reflected can be seen with a minimum of self-protective rationalization, then a pivotal dilemma can arise—indeed, will arise if what is seen is not what we imagined for ourselves back when we thought calmly about what we wanted to become.

Such a moment in a person's life constitutes a moral climax—a coming face-to-face with a self that is so inconsistent with our values that we must either turn away from self-reflection and witnessing altogether or, at last, change course. It is a pivotal moment in a person's life. And what Fuller argued is that such a moment now exists for humankind.[13]

In their book *The Lessons of History*, Will and Ariel Durant wrote, "The only real revolution is in the enlightenment of the mind and the improvement of character, the only real emancipation is individual, and the only real revolutionists are philosophers and saints."[14]

At its core, the focus of this book—and the training program discussed above—is on the individual, on the enlightenment of the mind and the improvement of character through conduct in accord with the ethics of human development. The focus is on a self that can effectively and ethically navigate the morality play that is life on this planet. The liberation that is both sought and required is from small-mindedness, from the frustrations and self-destructiveness of unruly and unconscious motivations, and from the sense of alienation and *cutoffness* that separate us from ourselves and others. This is not a book or a program that makes us philosophers or saints. It is, however, a book and program about self-development and social change, about assisting in the revolution of which the Durant's wrote.

E. F. Schumacher suggested that we need to see the world in a new light, "as a place where the things modern man continuously talks about and always fails to accomplish can actually be done."[15] The Earth is generous, he argued, and there is no reason for anyone to live in misery. Like Fuller, Schumacher believed that the know-how to make the world work for everyone exists and that more know-how is being developed daily. For Schumacher, Fuller's "network of unstable holding patterns held in place by ignorance and fear" is the ethical dilemma of our time.

An essential part of the answer to Schumacher's and Fuller's dilemma resides in the development of the conscious and ethical self. With that development, and offering the measure of it, come decisions and actions that leverage the future in humanity's favor—decisions and actions that, by degree, are driven less by ignorance and fear and more by reason, vision, and love; decisions made by individuals who can recognize an ethical/self-making dilemma when it presents itself and who can respond with more of humanity's welfare, life itself, in mind. These individuals have achieved a remarkable degree of self-mastery and with it a profound sense of life's possibility. They have realized and manifested through their actions one of the most important of all inherent possibilities: the ability to become and remain (as Wilshire put it) "aware, interpreting and free,"[16] valuing and serving the emergence of that same ability in others. This so that life can increasingly be valued first among competing concerns. And this so that life, the nature of being itself, can realize whatever inherent possibility resides within it.

SUMMARY

There are many legitimate approaches to addressing the dilemmas facing humankind. Here the focus is on the self-change that is invariably social change; the self-change that is certain to strengthen what Robert Wright calls "the fabric of mutual benefit."[17] The individual who pursues his maturity through conduct in accord with the ethics of human development cannot help but positively impact the organizations of which he or she is a part. The organization committed to building within itself an ethical culture cannot help but affect the development of its members. And this effort on the part of both inevitably affects the larger community, its center of gravity.

A community is simply a very large organization, made up of hundreds, even thousands of smaller organizations (not to mention the families that comprise it). How many of these smaller organizations must be actively engaged in building ethical cultures within themselves before the larger community begins to benefit from their effort? This is one way for communities to transform themselves. The focus is on the individual, on the complete energizing of our capacities as selves or persons. The unit of change, however, is twofold: both individual and organizational. As both benefit, so, too, does the larger community, since the larger community can only be as prosperous and as creative, as ecologically sane and life-embracing, as the character of its citizens and their organizations permit.

Afterword

"Justice, in the ethical sense, is giving to every [person] the indispensable conditions of self-realization."[1]

—Wilbur Marshall Urban
Fundamentals of Ethics

The preface of this book suggested that life can be viewed in any number of ways, but that here, it would be viewed as a morality play. One of the underlying assumptions of this book is that as individuals mature, that is, as they increase their ethical creativity, they are less likely to self-destruct, more likely to produce a future wherein they are inviting that same maturity in others. More likely to ensure that the play continues.

In his book, *Finite and Infinite Games: A Vision of Life as Play and Possibility*, James Carse draws the distinction between finite and infinite games, between finite and infinite players. Writes Carse: Infinite players know "that it is our vision, and not what we are viewing, that is limited."[2] The ethics of human development are meant to be ethics for infinite play, for behaving our way into an expanded vision, ethics for individuals who increasingly are creative, compassionate, able, open, and flexible. This sort of development on the part of us all is needed if we are to have any hope of discovering what the play we are in is about. And in the end, that is the question on our minds: *What is this play about?*

The answer, of course, is that we do not know. Our current level of understanding and our current level of development do not permit us an answer. It is obvious, however, that unless we stick around, we will never know the answer. Humanity must continue, through time and down the Yellow Brick Road if it is to grasp the storyline, the larger narrative— grasp and, if need be, shape, giving it a direction that ensures not only survival but joy and fulfillment, as well. That is the ultimate function of the ethics of human development or conduct in accord with human logic: to help shape the narrative so that the play continues. That is what we are doing whenever we ethically resolve our everyday dilemmas. We are shaping the narrative of self, workplace, and society, and so, to a degree, the narrative of the play itself.

Two assumptions underlie this book. First, we want to realize our potential, the full realization of inherent possibilities. Second, ethical conduct facilitates the emergence of that potential and provides evidence of it. Along the way, a third assumption was added: It is not madness to have utopian ideals. The non–zero sum game, the world working for everyone (as Buckminster Fuller was fond of putting it), the opportunity for all people to travel the Yellow Brick Road—these are conceptualizations or goals humanity rejects at its peril. And while it is hard to imagine how such goals can be reached, the cause is presumably served if we can establish a link between these goals and the life of the self amid its everyday travails. That has been the background purpose of this book: to provide that link, to show that the ethics of human development, the resolution of our everyday dilemmas, the pursuit of valued behavior, aim us in the direction of an ideal, a self-realization that strengthens the fabric of mutual regard. It is true that while some gains resulting from our efforts may be too small to measure or even notice, others are not, as the dilemmas we face come in all sizes. The cumulative effect of our effort, however, gives evidence of the fact that we are not indifferent to our own future or to the future of life in general, and that we are capable of behaving with the realization of inherent possibilities, long-run ideals, the infinite game in mind.

Notes

Preface

[1] Durant, Will, *The Mansions of Philosophy*. Garden City, NY: Garden City Publishing Co., 1929, p. 20.

[2] My apologies to the commentator in question. I do not have his name, and this is not an exact quote, rather the spirit of what I remember him saying. The comment was made during a discussion on the MacNeil/Lehrer PBS NewsHour following Roger's death.

[3] Tetsuro, Watsuji, *Rinrigaku (Ethics in Japan)*, translated by Yamamoto Seisaku and Robert E. Carter. Published by State University of New York Press, Albany, 1996, p.22.

[4] Throughout this book, the use of the term "self" is shorthand for person or individual, i.e., "the development of the self" synonymous with "the development of the person," "selfhood" synonymous with "personhood".

[5] Whitman, Walt. From "Carol of Words" in *Leaves of Grass*. Philadelphia: David McKay, 1900, p. 219.

[6] Savory, Allan, *Holistic Resource Management*. Covelo, CA: Island Press, 1988, p. 398.

[7] For a poetic expression of this same point, see O'Donohue, John, *Beauty: The Invisible Embrace* (New York: Harper Perennial, 2005, p. 47). "There is a wonderful urgency within things to realize the dream of their individual fulfillment; nothing is neutral, everything is on its way."

[8] See the work of John David Garcia. In particular, see *The Moral Society: A Rational Alternative to Death* (New York: The Julian Press, 1971) and *Creative Transformation: A Practical Guide for Maximizing Creativity* (Eugene, OR: Noetic Press and Ardmore, PA: Whitmore Publishing Company, 1991). Garcia's work in general and his identification of the ethics required for creative and evolutionary advance, along with his analysis of the relationship of ethics to bureaucracy, are brilliant accomplishments to which this book owes a great deal.

[9] Wilshire, Bruce, *The Much-at-Once: Music, Science, Ecstasy, The Body*. Fordham University Press, New York, 2016, p. 241.

Part I—*Human Development and the Yellow Brick Road*

[1] Schumacher, E. F., *A Guide for the Perplexed*. New York: Harper & Row, 1977, p. 132.

[2] The "Yellow Brick Road" is a key element in L. Frank Baum's novel *The Wizard of Oz*. Dorothy, Baum's central character, must travel the Yellow Brick Road if she has any hope of returning to her beloved home. Another use of the Yellow Brick Road can be found in Norman Spinrad's remarkable novel *Child of Fortune* (New York: Bantam Books, 1985). See for example p. xi: "But all too many adolescents in all too many cultures never passed through Chaos at all. They were born, they were acculturated, they were schooled, they took up their adult stations in life, passed through an ill-defined period of mid-life angst, resigned themselves to old age, and died, without ever walking the Yellow Brick Road, indeed without ever understanding what it was they had missed in their lives."

[3] Many such maps or systems depicting the stages of human development exist. See, for example, Schumacher (*A Guide for the Perplexed*); Ken Wilber (*Sex, Ecology and Spirituality: The Spirit of Evolution*, and in particular, *Integral Psychology*, in which Wilber presents and compares many developmental systems); Robert Kegan *(The Evolving Self)*; and Timothy Leary (*Exo-Psychology*). The system presented here was developed in 1983. It is from this system—working with it and using it as backdrop—that this book, and the ethics of human development, evolved. As for the origin of this system, I first developed the five levels (i.e., No Mind, Hive Mind, etc.) and began exploring ways of making that sequence useful as a way of describing human development. It was during that time that I read *The Mirror and the Lamp*, in which M. H. Abrams argues that the metaphor for the mind from Plato's time to the time of the Romantic poets was the mirror, at which point it became the lamp. I therefore aligned mirror with Hive Mind and lamp with Poetic Mind and began asking the questions that allowed me to flesh out the schematic. The schematic was completed in short order except for two entries. It was my colleague Dan Daly, PhD, who suggested that I use eagle for Heroic Mind and dolphin for Poetic Mind.

[4] This quote is found in a book entitled *Child* edited by Helen Handley and Andra Samelson (New York: Pushcart Press, 1988, p. 66) containing quotations from a variety of authors on the nature and experience of childhood.

[5] Wilber, *Integral Psychology*, pp. 47–53; Wilber, *Sex, Ecology, Spirituality*, pp. 51–54. Referring to the work of Don Beck/Spiral Dynamics, this is what Wilber calls "the Prime Directive, not preferential treatment of any one level" (*Integral Psychology*, p. 232). The problem, according to Wilber and others (*Integral Psychology*, pp. 230–32), is that prior to Level Five (excluding Level One)—I'm applying Wilber's point to my Five Levels—each level (or the mindset associated with each level) considers itself to have "arrived" and experiences the motives and worldview of other levels as error, threat, or both. The tension or battle between these levels of mind is played out on the evolutionary stage as each level views the others with varying degrees of fear, suspicion, and disdain. Only with maturity comes perspective, a compassion that allows each level its place within a developmental sequence. And though the other levels may view Level V with the same suspicion/disdain that they view one another, those who achieve Level V have one key motivational advantage: They know that their growth and continuing maturation depends in part on the development they are able to support in others. See also Colin Wilson's *Poetry and Mysticism* (San Francisco: City Lights Books, 1969, p. 201): "The real conflict in [human beings] is not between 'body' and 'spirit,' but between different levels of mind."

[6] Spinrad, Norman, *Child of Fortune*, p. 350.

[7] Carse, James, *Finite and Infinite Games*. New York: Ballantine Books, 1986, p. 144.

Part II—*Human Logic and the Ethics of Human Development*

[1] Urban, Wilbur Marshall, *Fundamentals of Ethics*. New York: Henry Holt and Company, 1939, p. 118.

[2] Garcia, *Creative Transformation*, p. 324.

[3] Both Ethic 2: The Open-Mindedness Ethic and Ethic 3: The Deliberate Action Ethic draw heavily on the work of John David Garcia. See for example *The Moral Society: A Rational Alternative to Death* (New York: The Julian Press, 1971, p. 1): "In the end, a person who is honest with himself always has doubts..." Garcia writes: "1) It is unethical to be certain; 2) it is ethical to doubt; and 3) inaction is unethical." In *Creative Transformation: A Practical Guide for Maximizing Creativity* (Eugene, OR: Noetic Press and Ardmore, PA: Whitmore Publishing Company, 1991), Garcia returns to this point (p. 306): "Our models of nature cannot evolve unless we doubt their validity." In *The Moral Society* (p. 140), Garcia adds a corollary to this argument: "It is unethical to give up hope because it is unethical to be certain."

[4] This is a point made repeatedly in the works of Wilber. See for example *Sex, Ecology, Spirituality: The Spirit of Evolution* (London & Boston: Shambhala Publications, 1995).

[5] Garcia, *The Moral Society*, p. 1: "The problem each person must solve for himself is how to act ethically when the future outcome of every act is uncertain."

[6] Again, Garcia offers guidance: "We should try to avoid any act which might result in irreversible damage if our judgment is in error, although it is better to act decisively than not to act at all." *Creative Transformation*, p. 152.

[7] Boal, Augusto, *Games for Actors and Non-Actors*. New York: Routledge, Chapman and Hall, 1992, p. xxv.

[8] Throughout both *The Moral Society* and *Creative Transformation*, Garcia emphasizes the importance of giving and receiving feedback. In *The Moral Society* (p. 38), he writes: "Deliberate destruction of feedback is always immoral." In *Creative Transformation* (p. 255): "The great challenge is to give negative feedback with love and humility and not with anger and arrogance."

[9] Garcia, *The Moral Society*, p. 31.

[10] As an aside, it is only through the inviting of feedback—the openness to and welcoming of feedback—that we realize that feedback is ever-present, that there is a continuous feedback loop between self and world. And though much of the feedback we receive is subtle and easily missed when one is in a "noisy" or distracted state of mind, it is there and helpful beyond measure—the continuous conversation, rapport, or dialogue between self and world that helps one define and perhaps expand the sense of self.

[11] Garcia, *Creative Transformation*, p. 270.

[12] Kegan, Robert, and Lahey, Lisa Laskow, *How the Way We Talk Can Change the Way We Work.* San Francisco: Jossey-Bass, 2001, p. 101. Kegan and Lahey write (p. 99): "If we characterize people, even if we do so quite positively, we actually engage—however unintentionally—in the rather presumptuous activity of entitling ourselves to say who and how the other is. We entitle ourselves to confer upon people the sources of their worthiness."

[13] Ibid, p. 101: "This is not what we mean by the language of ongoing regard. Ongoing regard is not about praising, stroking, or positively defining a person to herself or to others. We say again: it is about enhancing the quality of a precious kind of information. It is about informing the person about our experience of him or her."

[14] Peck, M. Scott, *The Road Less Traveled.* New York: Simon and Schuster, 1978, pp. 62-63.

[15] Schultz, Will, *Elements of Encounter.* Joy Press, 1973.

[16] The Enron debacle may a case in point. In that situation, truth was withheld for self-serving ends, withheld so a few could escape the collapsing edifice with their gains intact while others, excluded from the truth, were certain to lose everything. This caused outrage where before there had been trust. The understandable response to such a situation is an increase in policing, an increase in the network of regulations that ensure accountability so that all players—not just the few—are protected against one group taking advantage of another. This increase in regulation may be healthy, it may be what is needed, but it illustrates what happens when the trust built up through truth-telling (as well as through ethical performance in general) is broken. The environment becomes more complex, the ease of navigation that was possible when trust prevailed reduced.

[17] Lao Tsu, *The Tao Te Ching.* New York: Vintage Books, 1989, p. 65.

[18] Tolle, Eckhart, *The Power of Now.* Novato, CA: New World Library, 1999, p. 181.

[19] Garcia, *Creative Transformation,* pp. 257–58. Garcia writes: "In this belief, which I call the 'victim paradigm,' the persons are denying their free will... There is nothing more destructive that persons can do to themselves."
Also, see Urban in *Fundamentals of Ethics* (p. 159): "The life of every man is a continuous process of choice. Even the refusal to choose, as William James was fond of pointing out, is itself a form of choice. No one can escape this fundamental character of human life, for it lies in the very nature of the life process itself." And p. 394: "The moral life is a continuous process of choice—of choice of one value over another and of choice of acts leading to the realization of the chosen values. The question immediately arises whether this choice is real or only apparent, whether the will is free or actually determined. When the philosopher thinks things out, he cannot avoid the conclusion that if the moral life is to have any meaning at all, freedom of the will must be real." And p. 360: "For the [scientist] it seems, for instance, that for the universe to be rational it must be determined, and so the scientist seeks to find law and determinism in it. For morality, on the other hand, a rational universe must be one in which freedom is possible, so the moral philosopher seeks to find freedom in it. There is no real reason why one procedure should be 'rationalization' in the bad sense any more than the other. The philosopher at least refuses to start with either prejudice. Perhaps when he thinks things through, he will find both positions to have their element of truth. This at least is the possibility with which the philosopher starts. It is possible that it is also the conclusion to which he will finally come."

[20] Berger, Peter, *Invitation to Sociology: A Humanistic Perspective.* Garden City, NY: Doubleday & Co., 1963, p. 143.

[21] Miller, L. Keith, University of Kansas. Personal communication.

[22] Perhaps there is yet another step we can take with this challenging but critical ethic. Put it this way: Yes, you have choice and as you so choose, it is possible to take yourself to the place *where there is no choice at all.* This takes effort, discipline, commitment to the realization of our highest possibility, the freedom from choice altogether as choice yields, as Iris Murdoch's suggests in her book, *The Sovereignty of Good,* to something akin to obedience.
Each moment as it is defined by all that makes it up... each moment when fully grasped calls for a single response. One response (though its form may vary) that is right, true, good, a proper ethical fit. This is the realm of the saint, the life artist... discernment and development of that degree a rare achievement.
Until that level of development is achieved, however, that level of awareness, sensitivity, selflessness, until then, we are in the dark. And so, the burden of choice. We choose our way forward, anchoring our choices to our values with the hope (unconscious or otherwise) that clarity will result. And with it, freedom from confusion about what we must do, the courage to act the only choice remaining and that choice, by then, with such clarity at hand, hardly an issue.
This I take to be what Iris Murdoch is arguing in *Sovereignty.* *"If I attend properly, I will have no choice and this is the ultimate condition to be aimed at. ...The ideal situation... to be represented as a kind of 'necessity'."* Murdoch, Iris, *The Sovereignty of Good.* London: Routledge Classics, 2001, pgs. 38-39. Something similar is being said by Wilshire, *The*

Much at Once, p. 90: *"No 'free will' drops down from the sky as an undeserved gift. We must work and endure and allow certain impulses to happen if we are to be the effective free agents that at times we certainly seem to be. Freedom requires the willingness and ability to do the valuable thing or to let it happen: As Emerson would say, the ability at crucial moments to abandon calculation, the attempt to totally control. ...The real meaning of freedom is allowing powerful creative processes to grip, pull, propel, and direct us."*

[23] Schumacher, E. F., *Small is Beautiful: Economics As If People Mattered.* New York: Harper & Row Publishers, 1973. Also, see Schumacher's essay entitled, "Buddhist Economics". Parabola, Vol. 16, No. 1, Spring 1991: "It is clear, therefore, that Buddhist economics must be very different from the economics of modern materialism, since the Buddhist sees the essence of civilization not in a multiplication of wants but in the purification of human character. Character, at the same time, is formed primarily by a man's work. And work, properly conducted in conditions of human dignity and freedom, blesses those who do it and equally their products."

[24] Garcia, *The Moral Society*, p. 37: "To be ethical means that a person will correct his mistakes when they are perceived and that he will not deliberately blind himself to them."

[25] From an interview with Chuck Berry in *Hail, Hail, Rock & Roll*, a documentary film by director Taylor Hackford, 1987.

[26] See in this regard, Wilshire, Bruce, *Fashionable Nihilism.* State University of New York Press, Albany, 2001, p. 4. "Hegel put it succinctly: *Wesen ist was ist gewesen.* Being is what has become. Not to know how one has become what one is, means one has a grossly inadequate idea of what one is."

[27] There are, of course, what might be considered positive addictions such as exercise, meditation, one's creative activity, activities that do not make us weaker but strengthen us. This is the point that physician William Glasser makes in his book, *Positive Addiction.* New York: Harper & Row, Publishers, 1976. Bruce Wilshire makes a similar point in *Wild Hunger: The Primal Roots of Modern Addiction.* New York: Rowman & Littlefield Publishers, 1998. Wilshire writes (pp. 98-99): ". . . the withdrawal symptom criterion includes within the class of addictive behaviors those that should not be called that at all. Take ardent mountain climbing or an all-absorbing artistic career or serious playing of any sort. Very difficult it is to give these up, and if they were to be withdrawn, distress would occur." Even so, Wilshire points out, these activities feed us, giving us more than they take away. The addiction discussed in the text, however, is the addiction arrived at primarily through conscious mistakes, through the conscious choosing of the option that at some level is recognized as self-destructive. This is the addiction that takes away more than it gives, weakening the capacity for choice while also narrowing the range of options from which one might choose.

[28] Concerning the issue of conscious mistakes: What about the map or worldview that insists that violence be done to others? How else are we to achieve our ends, our dreams? How else do we secure our revenge? Some cultures or subcultures or individuals may think it so. Indeed, history, one might argue, is the story of violent overtaking, one individual or group by another. *That's how we got here.* Are we to engage in violence if it is integral to our worldview or map, a conscious mistake if we do not? Perhaps. Horrible circumstances do arise. Conflicts go primal and violence results and is perpetuated. After all, it is us or them. A conscious mistake not to prevail. This is primal logic. Survival logic. And we are animals. However, we are pursuing another kind of logic, *human logic,* with self-realization and human flourishing its aim. Survival is not threatened. Emergency and alarm are not coursing through the nervous system. A relative degree of peace exists (and, for most of us, is required) for individuals to consider what is required for the realization of inherent possibilities and violence is not likely to be considered a legitimate means. Too much blowback, retribution, and psychic damage comes with it. Perhaps history, whatever else it is, is also the slow clearing of the ground... permitting room for more and more people to live and create in accord with human logic. The ethics of human development in their entirety are peace-making ethics and are incompatible with violence toward others.

[29] Carey, Ken. Tape presentation of his book *The Third Millennium: Living in the Posthistoric World.* New York: HarperCollins, 1991.

[30] Urban, *Fundamentals of Ethics*, p. 454.

[31] Urban quotes Tennyson in *Fundamentals of Ethics*, pp. 423–24: "And I doubt not through the ages one increasing purpose runs."

[32] Platt, John R, "Social Traps." In *American Psychologist*, Vol. 28, No. 8, August 1973, pp. 641–51.

[33] Hardin, Garrett, "The Tragedy of the Commons." In *Science*, Vol. 162, 1968, pp. 1,243–48.

[34] Platt, "Social Traps," p. 643.

[35] Rachlin, Howard, and Green, Leonard, "Commitment, Choice and Self-Control." In the *Journal of the Experimental Analysis of Behavior*, Vol. 17, 1972, pp. 15–22.

[36] Hardin, Garrett, *Exploring New Ethics for Survival: The Voyage of the Spaceship Beagle.* New York: Viking Press, 1972, pp. 18–19.

[37] Platt, "Social Traps," p. 650.

[38] Hardin, *Exploring New Ethics for Survival*, pp. 77–87.

[39] See Ostrom, Elinor, *Governing the Commons: The Evolution of Institutions for Collective Action.* Cambridge, United Kingdom: Cambridge University Press, 2003. Ostrom surveys a variety of models and methods utilized by organizations and by individuals operating voluntarily to manage shared resources.

[40] The work of psychologist Lawrence Kohlberg focused on moral development and on what he considered the stages of moral development; see L. Kohlberg, "Moral Development and Identification," in *Yearbook*, National Society for the Study of Education, 1962. See also Arthur J. Deikman, *The Observing Self: Mysticism and Psychotherapy* (Boston: Beacon Press, 1982, pp. 85–89). Kohlberg argued that individuals pass through a sequence of moral development stages: the egocentric stage, for example, in which self-identity extends to the boundary of the skin and not much further, where the focus of moral concern is on "my needs," "my wishes," "my survival"; the ethnocentric stage, in which self-identity expands to include one's clan, tribe, community, or nation, with the focus of moral concern expanded to include "my clan's needs, wishes, and requirements"; and the worldcentric stage, in which self-identity expands to all people everywhere, the focus of the individual's concern now on what is needed in order for all people to survive and prosper. Conduct, Kohlberg argued, aligns with the stage at which the individual finds herself, a point frequently made in the writings of Ken Wilber. Wilber notes that society would be wise to organize with this fact in mind, building in the supports that help ensure conduct that does not harm society while at the same time allowing the individual the time needed to develop and mature. This same point is recognized by the field known as Applied Behavior Analysis, though the notion of "stages as internal, unfolding structures" would be discarded in favor simply of an analysis of what the individual can and cannot do. If the desired behavior is absent (in this case, for example, behavior consistent with worldcentric concerns), then the "contingencies of reinforcement" present in the environment are rearranged to shape and maintain the desired behavior until the individual can maintain the behavior on her own. The purpose of Applied Behavior Analysis being, in part, to help individuals acquire the capacity to behave in accord with long-term desired ends though the current environment does not support it (L. Keith Miller, University of Kansas, personal communication). Related to this last point, see Rachlin, Howard, *The Escape of the Mind*, Oxford University Press, 2014, p. 114: "When people act for the long-term good of themselves and their society, in cases where such acts conflict with their immediate and individual pleasures, they may meaningfully be said to be acting freely; …A person who does this is free from particular influences in the same sense that an ocean liner is free from the influence of small waves."

[41] For more on the idea of the Wind Harp, see Barfield, *The Rediscovery of Meaning*, pp. 65–78.

[42] Miller, Alice, *The Drama of the Gifted Child.* New York: Basic Books, 1981.

[43] Gandhi's actual statement, frequently quoted, was: "Be the change you would like to see in others."

[44] Garcia, *Creative Transformation*, as well as his online publications at www. see.org/garcia/.

[45] This ethic, as with others already mentioned, owes much to the writings of Garcia. This point in particular—that we have an ethical requirement to share our gift with at least one other person for their benefit—is Garcia's.

[46] Fuller, Buckminster, "The Fifty-Year Experiment." An audio tape published by New Dimensions, San Francisco, 1982. This is a slight modification in the wording of Fuller's statement.

[47] Hyde, Lewis, *The Gift: Imagination and the Erotic Life of Property.* New York: Vintage Books, 1983, pp. 35–39.

[48] Ibid, pp. 38–39, 74–75, 78, 153, 194.

[49] Ibid, p. 25.

⁵⁰ Lao Tsu, *Tao Te Ching*, translated by Gia-Fu Feng and Jane English, introduction by Jacob Needleman. New York: Vantage Books, 1989, p. xiv.

⁵¹ Fuller, Buckminster, *Cosmography: A Posthumous Scenario for the Future of Humanity*. New York: Macmillan Publishing Co., 1992, p. 117.

Part III—*Dilemmas from Everyday Life*

[1] Hillenbrand, Laura. *Seabiscuit: An American Legend.* New York: Random House, 2001, p. 106.

[2] Garcia, *Creative Transformation*, p. 270.

[3] In an article entitled, "Perspectives on Selfhood", psychologist M. Brewster Smith discussed the nature of selfhood, what it is and how it might be acquired. Concerning its features, Smith writes: "... Selfhood involves being self-aware or reflective; being or having a body... somehow taking into account the boundaries of selfhood at birth and death and feeling a continuity of identity in between; placing oneself in a generational sequence and network of other connected selves as forebears and descendants and relatives; being in partial communication and communion with other contemporary selves while experiencing an irreducible separateness of experience and identity; engaging in joint and individual enterprises in the world with some degree of forethought and afterthought (not just "behaving"); guiding what one does and appraising what one has done at least partly through reflection on one's performance; feeling responsible, at least sometimes, for one's actions and holding others responsible for theirs." *American Psychologist,* 1978, *33,* 1053-1063.   The aspects of selfhood emphasized in the text are self-awareness, self-review, the continuity of identity, the holding of oneself responsible for one's actions, engaging in joint and individual enterprises in the world with some degree of forethought and afterthought (not just "behaving").

[4] Deikman, *The Observing Self.*

[5] Ibid., pp. 94–96.

[6] Psychologist Steven Hayes argues that through the acquisition of language, the observing self is made as the individual learns to distinguish between I/you, here/there, now/then. As Hayes points out, *I, here*, and *now* characterize (or are true for) all observations made throughout an individual's lifetime. In that sense, writes Hayes, "the 'I' is boundless (or is experienced as such)"; not bounded by time or space since the "I" is always present whenever and wherever observations occur. See Steven C. Hayes's *Get Out of Your Mind & Into Your Life: The New Acceptance & Commitment Therapy* (Oakland, CA: New Harbinger Publications, 2005, pp. 94–95).

[7] In his book, *The Illusion of Technique* (New York: Anchor Books, 1973, p. 322), William Barrett addresses the issue of being and becoming, or Being and doing, as he puts it. His conclusion: "The truth of human life must perpetually lie in the tension between Being and doing. We can never resolve the question exclusively in favor of one or the other side. All our doing must take place within the context of Being, with its mystery present and alive to us. Otherwise, we are simply scurrying around aimlessly in the mazes of our own contrivances. On the other hand, to seek absorption in Being, as an escape from the tasks of ordinary life, can only lead to quiescence and boring repletion. Man is the creature who must live in perpetual tension between these opposites. He is their tension and copresence."

[8] Wilshire, Bruce. *Role Playing and Identity: The Limits of Theatre as Metaphor.* Bloomington, IN: Indiana University Press, pp. xiii, 14, 272.

[9] From "Don Juan in Hell," Act III from *Man and Superman* by George Bernard Shaw; see www.bigeye.com/donjuan.htm.

[10] Hurston, Zora Neale, *Their Eyes Were Watching God.* New York: HarperCollins Publishers, 1990, pp. 8–9.

[11] Schumacher, *A Guide for the Perplexed*, p. 83.

[12] Whitman's epic poem *Leaves of Grass* is both exercise and celebration of this point, the moral imagination expanded until self-identity includes all people in all ways of life. "In all people I see myself—none more, and not one a barleycorn less; / And the good or bad I say of myself, I say of them." *Leaves of Grass*, Mineola, NY: Dover Publications, 2007, p. 35.

[13] This scene was inspired by—and is a slight modification of—a scene from *The West Wing*, a television series that aired from 1999 to 2006, created by Aaron Sorkin. See http://en.wikipedia.org/wiki/The_West_Wing.

[14] See the works of Ken Keyes Jr., in particular *Handbook of Higher Consciousness*, Berkeley, CA: Living Love Center, 1975.

[15] Kimmerer, Robin Wall, *Braiding Sweetgrass.* Milkweed Editions, Minneapolis, Minnesota, 2013, p. 15.

Part IV— *Consciousness, Valued Behavior & the Center of Gravity*

[1] Murdoch, Iris, *The Sovereignty of Good.* London: Routledge Classics, 2001, p. 82.

[2] Rachlin, Howard, *The Escape of the Mind.* Oxford University Press, 2014, pg. 152-153. "...we can get at least a basic understanding of the nature of consciousness by considering what is called intentionality. ... Intentionality refers to the phenomenal fact that consciousness always seems to have an object. Consciousness is not an entity on its own... it is a process or action... It will be helpful to keep in mind the Husserlian motto: consciousness is always consciousness *of* something."

[3] Murdoch, pp. 54-55.

[4] Schumacher, *A Guide for the Perplexed*, p. 72.

[5] Ibid, p. 72.

[6] Hayes and his colleagues have developed numerous techniques for this purpose – see *Get Out of Your Mind & Into Your Life.*

[7] In this connection, I want to acknowledge the work of Maria Nemeth, PhD. See *Mastering Life's Energies: Simple Steps to a Luminous Life at Work and Play* (Novato, CA: New World Library, 2007). Also, Hayes, *Get Out of Your Mind & Into Your Life.*

[8] Hayes, p. 10. For Hayes, the prospect of suffering is an inevitable byproduct of the fact that human beings have language and, thus, the capacity to think relationally. Humans can relate the most beautiful, joyful event to the absence of a loved one and suddenly the event becomes unbearably sad. Hayes argues that this capacity—to relate anything to anything— makes possible both remarkable problem-solving capacity and inevitable suffering. We are conscious of what and whom we have lost; conscious also of the discomfort, injustice, and injury we have seen and perhaps endured. And all of this is woven together with language, recall, our capacity to associate anything with anything, thus making suffering an almost certain part of human experience.

[9] Ibid, pp. 165–91.

[10] Ibid.

[11] Hayes and his colleagues have developed several techniques for viewing thoughts and separating oneself from the thoughts one thinks. These techniques are collectively known as defusion. "Cognitive defusion techniques . . ." writes Hayes, "help you make the distinction between the world as structured by your thoughts and thinking as an ongoing process. When your thoughts are about you yourself, defusion can help you to distinguish between the person doing the thinking and the verbal categories you apply to yourself through thinking," (Hayes, *Get Out of Your Mind*, p. 69). And again, "When you think a thought, it structures your world. When you see a thought, you can still see how it structures your world (you understand what it means), but you also see that you are doing the structuring. That awareness gives you a little more room for flexibility" (p. 71).

[12] Hayes, pp. 153–54, 197.

[13] Wilber, *A Brief History of Everything*, p. 139.

Part V— *The Theater of Change*

[1] Wilshire, *Role Playing and Identity,* pp. ix–x.

[2] Boal, Augusto, *Games for Actors and Non-Actors.*

[3] See the works of Virginia Satir, including *Conjoint Family Therapy* (Palo Alto, CA: Science and Behavior Books, 1983); *The New Peoplemaking* (Palo Alto, CA: Science and Behavior Books, 1988); *The Satir Model: Family Therapy and Beyond* (Palo Alto, CA: Science and Behavior Books, 1991).

[4] The role-playing procedure follows a modification of Boal's model developed by Douglas Paterson, Professor of Dramatic Arts at the University of Nebraska/Omaha.

[5] Wilshire, p. 11.

[6] Wilshire, p. 152: "It can be argued that it took philosophy over two thousand years, until Hegel, to reach this insight: a human being can become itself, its self, only when it makes its own what others have made of it." And again (p. 204): "...the life-actor like the stage actor must make his own to ever greater degrees what others have made of him."

[7] Mead, G. H. "A Behavioristic Account of the Significant Symbol." *Journal of Philosophy,* Vol. XIX, 1922. This appears as a footnote in Wilshire, *Role Playing and Identity*, p. 166.

[8] Quoted in Will Durant's *The Story of Philosophy: The Lives and Opinions of the World's Greatest Philosophers.* New York: Simon & Schuster, 1961, p. 312.

[9] Becker, Ernest, *The Denial of Death.* New York: The Free Press, 1973, p. 183.

[10] I believe this phrase should be attributed to Urban, *Fundamentals of Ethics*.

[11] Fuller, R. Buckminster. *Critical Path.* New York: St. Martin's Press, 1981.

[12] Wilshire, *Role Playing and Identity*, p. 204: "One is returned to himself augmented, confirmed, and perhaps clarified by the other. One has left his mark on the other and through him upon oneself—l'effet c'est moi!—the effect, it is I!"

[13] Is that so? Is Fuller's Utopia or Oblivion too severe? There is the climate crisis. There is nuclear proliferation making even more dangerous the clash of cultures, ideologies, and isms throughout the world. Aggravating this mix of factors is severe inequality, poverty, institutions that are challenged and, in many cases, no longer trusted. There is the continuous threat of a pandemic for which we may or may not be prepared. And there is the danger of AI. At the same time, there is science, technology, and the promise of AI. There is the creative spirit and the brilliant minds working on innovative solutions. There is the work of so many summarized in Steven Pinker's book, *Enlightenment NOW: The Case for Reason, Science, Humanism, and Progress* (New York, Viking Press, 2018) indicating that many key indicators of human wellbeing have been improving continuously, that life is getting better for more and more people. Since the publication of that book, many disruptive events have occurred. Still, we must ask again and again and be open to—and I would think be guided by—what the data say! Whatever the true picture of our current moment, the ethics of human development remain relevant, a society with institutions anchored to human logic the aim. This prepares us for and perhaps makes less likely the self-destruction that Fuller feared could be in the offing.

[14] Durant, Will and Ariel. *The Lessons of History.* New York: Simon and Schuster, 1968, p. 72.

[15] Schumacher, *A Guide for the Perplexed*, p. 139.

[16] Wilshire, *Role Playing and Identity*, p. xii.

[17] Wright, Robert. *Nonzero: The Logic of Human Destiny.* New York: Vintage Books, 2000, p. 135.

Afterword

[1] Urban, *Fundamentals of Ethics*, p. 225.

[2] Carse, James, *Finite and Infinite Games: A Vision of Life as Play and Possibility,* p. 75.

For more on *The Ethics of Human Development Training Program* including the "Complete Guide" containing training materials and methods, go to davidthomasphd.com.